Books by D. A. Powell

Tea

Lunch

Cocktails

Chronic

By Myself: An Autobiography
(with David Trinidad)

Useless Landscape, or A Guide for Boys

Repast

TEA

LUNCH

COCKTAILS

D. A. Powell

Graywolf Press

Two sections in *Repast* were originally published as the books *Tea* (1998) and *Lunch* (2000). They are published here by arrangement with Wesleyan University Press. *Cocktails* was originally published by Graywolf Press in 2004.

This publication is made possible, in part, by the voters of Minnesota through a Minnesota State Arts Board Operating Support grant, thanks to a legislative appropriation from the arts and cultural heritage fund, and through a grant from the Wells Fargo Foundation Minnesota. Significant support has also been provided by Target, the McKnight Foundation, Amazon.com, and other generous contributions from foundations, corporations, and individuals. To these organizations and individuals we offer our heartfelt thanks.

Published by Graywolf Press
250 Third Avenue North, Suite 600
Minneapolis, Minnesota 55401

www.graywolfpress.org

Published in the United States of America

ISBN 978-1-55597-696-5

2 4 6 8   9 7 5 3 1
First Graywolf Printing, 2014

Library of Congress Control Number: 2014935838

Cover design: Kyle G. Hunter

Cover art:
Black leather background: Ursula Alter / E+ / Getty Images;
Teacup and silverware: Shutterstock;
Cocktail umbrella: CSA Images / B&W Engrave Ink Collection / Vetta / Getty Images

CONTENTS

Spilling Tea

Tea Rooms

Reading Tea

Lunch

Softly and Tenderly

Sweet By and By

Gather at the River

In the Middle of the Air

Cocktails

Mixology

Filmography

Bibliography

INTRODUCTION: the sad part of living is eating and dying

In 1998, just as marriage equality was beginning to supplant Aids as the main preoccupation of politi-
cally minded gay people, a poet named D. A. Powell erupted into publication with a collection called *Tea*.
"Because I was unable to contain the first lines I wrote," Powell explained in the introduction, "I turned my
notebook sideways, pushing into what would traditionally be the margins of the page." The result was a book
that challenged the conventions of printing as well as poetic form. With its bracketed, lowercase non-titles,
its wide lines occasionally interrupted by graphics, its triple spaces like heavy breathing, *Tea* announced
the arrival of what Harold Bloom calls a "strong" poet—one whose originality derives from and reflects a
tradition that he is challenging even as he adds to it. Shakespeare is everywhere in *Tea*'s oversize pages. So
are Walt Whitman and Gertrude Stein. So are Robert Duncan and Gary Soto, poets who, like Powell, grew
up in California's Central Valley. Yet just as important to him are such iconic figures of the disco era as
Sylvester, the Weather Girls, Bonnie Pointer, Sheila E., and Vivien Vee. In one of my favorite poems in *Tea,*
Powell speaks in the voice of Regan MacNeil, the little girl played by Linda Blair in *The Exorcist*:

he'd make my bed jumble and squeak.   a parrot must have lit inside.   potty mouthed

I wouldn't have said, "quaquaquaquaqua" but his fingers pushed the dark: sores raised like letters

As it happens, the demonic lover—bearing both tricks and treats—is a recurring figure in Powell's
poetry, reaching his apotheosis in the malevolent and sexy "father xmas" in a poem for which Eartha
Kitt's "Santa, Baby" is the inspiration:

when you touch down upon this earth.   little reindeers
hoofing murderously at the gray slate roof: I lie beneath
dearest father xmas: will you bring me another 17 years

you gave me my first tin star and my first tin wreath
warm socks tangerines and a sloppy midnight kiss
I left you tollhouse cookies.   you left me bloody briefs

This poem is from *Cocktails,* Powell's third collection, published in 2004 and comprising, with *Tea* and
Lunch (2000), the trilogy gathered here. "This is not a book about Aids," he writes in the introduction to

Tea—a sentiment that extends to all three volumes. "I offer this at the outset, because I know that in the short-hand way in which books are discussed, catalogued, reviewed, marketed, introduced, Aids will inevitably be touted as one of the cries of the book's occasion. I do not deny this disease its impact. But I deny its dominion."

Right on. In his poems about Aids, Powell, to his great credit, refuses to play to the gallery. Instead he mixes gay slang, horror-movie kitsch, shudder-inducing eroticism, and a vocabulary to rival that of Norman Rush into a cocktail guaranteed to leave the reader punch-drunk, a lunch in the wake of which you won't want to contemplate supper. Here is Powell's disarming little time-bomb of a poem about someone getting the news that he is HIV-positive:

> you don't have syphilis.   the doctor says
> you don't have hepatitis.   he says
> you aren't diabetic.   the doctor says
>
> cholesterol level normal.   blood pressure
> good.   he says you've got great reflexes
> the doctor says these things.   he's the doctor
>
> he says I *do* have a bit of bad news.   he says
> just like that: I *do* have a bit of bad news
> not a *real* doctor remember: a physician's *assistant*

And here Powell is on hope, the snake oil of our time:

> I make hope the size of a bar of soap: hope-on-a-rope
> like "hope there's not a spider in the shower this morning"
>
> "hope some broadway producer brings back *starlight express*"
> "maybe figs will be available fresh for a longer season
>
> [without the global warming, I should add, in case god listens]"
>
> and "maybe sheila e. will release a disc as good as *the glamorous life*"

Reading these lines—and so many others of Powell's—I am reminded of a sentence from Joy Williams's essay "Why I Write": "Good writing never soothes or comforts. It is no prescription, neither is it diversionary, although it can and should enchant while it explodes in the reader's face." Yet Powell, for all his skill at wielding literary TNT, is also a great lyric poet, as evidenced by the lovely, rigorous poems about childhood and the natural world that crop up intermittently in this trilogy, as if to assure us of the vastness of his range:

autumn set us heavily to task: unrooted the dahlias
lay wrapped in the cellar.   cider pressing time.   grain milling
time to pick persimmons.   time to fix the leaky hayloft

slaughtering time.   rendering time.   time to put up chokecherries
take the woolens from the cedar chest: britches mending time
rabbit hunting time.   tallow candle dipping time.   soap making time

On other occasions, he is wonderfully epigrammatic, evoking Emily Dickinson:

the sad part of living is eating and dying
our dialogue breaks off mid-sentence

the bill arrives as a eulogy: itemized
everyone swallows a breathmint.   repression

nevermind the cost: I'll pick up your tab
you got the cab.   these days green and folding

My own favorite poems in the Powell canon are those that take movies as their starting point. Who else but he could use *The Poseidon Adventure* as an opportunity to describe an event—seroconversion—that literally turns the narrator's life upside-down?

you couldn't know the disaster this voyage has been.   the *shvimen,* the *shvitzen*
yard by yard the little deaths accrued   [imagine your twin towers over and over and]

out: that glorious sky darkly hung with newspaper lanterns.   scalpel-shaped chimes

—what am I meaning to tell in this cramped space?   bubble suspended in glass—
the reckoning beyond this cargo hold.   dear god, who hears the pounding on the hull

Repast is the cunning title under which Powell has brought together these three early volumes. Most Powell titles do double duty—his cocktails are both drinks with parasols and those mixtures of medications by means of which people diagnosed with Aids may survive—and this one is no exception. Of course a repast is a feast, and there is plenty of feasting here, bacchanals in which appetite is its own object and from which the narrator emerges, more often than not, hungrier than he arrived. At the same time, the word *repast* suggests the idea of revisiting the past, of re-passing, of a *re-past,* perfect or imperfect ("how life imitates 'imitation of life,'" one of his narrators says). It is the repast that Powell's poems defiantly celebrate:

water doesn't hold our place: one day
we set down the long russian novel we've been ~~living~~ [writing?]

and the names of the characters blur.   the plot
becomes completely twisted: the way we once forgot

the names of the 7 dwarves.   also the dog's birthday also
a luncheon with kind aunt sarah.   and when we return

a child has folded the pages into paper sailboats
look: little rudderless skiffs listing and drifting

time to abandon this silly regatta.   time to skip stones

In Powell's universe, even mourning must be a form of celebration, even loss an occasion for the expression of joy.

—David Leavitt, 2014

Tea

THE TEA ON TEA

This is not a book about Aids. I offer this at the outset, because I know that in the short-hand way in which books are discussed, catalogued, reviewed, marketed, introduced, Aids will inevitably be touted as one of the cries of the book's occasion. I do not deny this disease its impact. But I deny its dominion.

I began *Tea* as a chronicle of a relationship. Having not written for a year following the relationship's terminus, I was compelled to begin writing again, and I took my failed relationship as subject. Because I was unable to contain the first lines I wrote, I turned my notebook sideways, pushing into what would traditionally be the margins of the page. These lines, with their peculiar leaps and awkward silences, became the strangely apt vessel into which I could pour my thoughts. I took fragments and made new statements from them, just as I wished to reshape my life from its incomplete bits.

For every thought I had of Scott in writing the first poems, I had as many thoughts of other loves—friends, lovers, "tricks"—who had passed through my life. And so I wrote of them also, reenacting the serial polygamy that had characterized my life. I do not mean for this condition to signify anyone's experience but my own: I had moved through the world a sexual libertine, unfaithful even in the way I conflated the touch of one lover with thoughts about another.

As memory required me to revisit the deaths of many of these men, I realized that I ran the danger of writing a collection in which death was a consequence of my "lifestyle." (I use quotes here, because I do not really understand the difference between a life and a lifestyle, aside from the fingerpointing. I am nevertheless happy to be accused of the style.) Some who read or who do not read this book will hold that opinion. But the truth was—is—that my life is a consequence of those deaths. My relationship with Scott was in part a failure of our understanding of the times. Our fear of knowing our own HIV status was one of the powerful forces that held us together and drove us apart: we saw each other alternately as the possibility of salvation and as the possible instrument of destruction. Because of this, we simultaneously loved and hated each other with a kind of emotional violence.

While I was writing these poems, a well-known poet, who is also queer, cautioned me against "using Aids as a metaphor for a consumptive relationship." I do not understand "metaphor." I have the sort of mind that lumps together odd events, that enjoys the simultaneity of experience. My parents divorced during the Watergate hearings. The backlash against disco coincided with the Reagan administration. I was hospitalized for a nearly fatal accident while my friend Andy was dying, the first of many I would lose to Aids. If two objects occupy the same space, is one a metaphor for the other? If so, then life is the cause of death; love, the root of unhappiness.

Yet there is a way in which Aids moves through the text, just as other forces, events, and characters move through it. Because I based these poems on my own experience, I had to uncover the subject that drove the writing; and so I had to walk down many corridors in order to find what was at center. Along the way, I had to write about failed love, destitution, prostitution, disease, homelessness, and a myriad other subjects in order to discover that the true hero of the poems is survival. This is how I came to put the elegies at the front of the book. I rise out of ashes. To survive is an astonishing gift. The price of that gift is memory.

~

The title of the book may puzzle some. Before I wrote *Tea* I had written a collection entitled *Lunch*. *Tea* seemed to be the next logical step. I chose tea as a central figure not only for this reason, but also because it has such wonderful resonance for me. "Tea" was a term from pre-Stonewall days that is still a part of the queer argot. Originally, when queers still referred to ourselves as "queens," "having tea" was a natural extension of one's royal masquerade. However, "tea" the beverage was not necessarily involved in "having tea." Instead, "tea" was a session of gossip exchange. If one was invited to "tea," this usually meant that one was going to be privy to some scandalous information.

A public area in which men gathered for sex (and gossip too) was hence a "tea room." And the last trip to the bars before the weekend ended—on Sunday afternoons—became the "tea dance." *Tea.* A wonderfully glamorous word to adorn rather unglamorous rituals.

With all of these coded meanings, I suppose one might be tempted to read the title as a furtive gesture. I did not intend to be furtive. Rather, I wished to bring into the language of the poems all of the kinds of speech that I have heard around me—tall speech and short speech, the proper and the vernacular. I honor my dead in the attempt to recapture their voices.

~

Despite any hardship, I see what a blessing my life has been. I have written this book for the men who did not live to write their own stories: David Damon, Ricky Encinas, Michael Montero, Fidel Bady, Daehn Lebhardt, Lewis Friedman, Victor Martinez, Nick Wilson, Ken Penny, Andy Moore, Jeff Mahoney, Jon Burnett, Ernie Lopes, Sylvester James, Gary Deal: a list that once begun has resisted closure. This is not about being queer and dying. It is about being human and living.

—D. A. Powell, 1997

Tea Leaves

Such are the final, unenviable forms that survival assumes.

—Marcel Proust, *The Past Recaptured*

[to end and to open with a field: andy buried under a hunter's moon. deer born of headlights]

to end and to open with a field: andy buried under a hunter's moon.   deer born of headlights
I had meant to be first among us dead.   swerve toward atonal tinkle of glass.   powerpole

death puked me back out of its paunch: indigestible clump.   naked and suffering the return of sense

in a separate ward andy made no smash: wrack of lung.   scrap of chassis.   towed to the yard

what cried out in the woods between us.   the owl that shrieked: I was the one who shined into the ground
the ground refused me.   the ground that would leave the easy prey to be scavenged and take and take

9

[gary asleep in his recliner. this prison work clobbers him. today let the men stand unguarded]

gary asleep in his recliner.   this prison work clobbers him.   today let the men stand unguarded
he is overwhelmed by his own cells.   a furtive shiv behind his eyes: searchbeams opaque and anil

he dreams a wall: desert beyond where nothing is not jagged or barbed.   breathing hard he scales
hands numb nopales: swollen but withering inward nerveless.   the sensation of pinpricks

one long last watch: ectomorphic lockdown.   he draws the early pension.   incomplete his sentence

[nicholas the ridiculous: you will always be 27 and impossible. no more expectations]

nicholas the ridiculous: you will always be 27 and impossible.   no more expectations
you didn't carry those who went in long cars after you.   stacking lie upon lie as with children
swearing "no" to pain and "yes" to eternity.   you would have been a bastard: told the truth

afternoons I knelt beside your hiding place   [this is the part where you speak to me from beyond]
and he walks with me and he talks with me.   he tells me that I am his own.   dammit
nothing.   oh sure once in a while a dream.   a half-instant.   but you are no angel you are

repeating the same episodes: nick at night.   tricky nick.   nicholas at halloween a giant tampon
don't make me mature by myself: redundancy of losing common ground.   for once be serious

[kenny lost in *the mineshaft* among silver stalactites. his irises bloom in darkness]

> I would give up all my life for just one kiss, I would surely die . . .
> —Freddie Mercury, "You Take My Breath Away"

kenny lost in *the mineshaft* among silver stalactites.   his irises bloom in darkness
the night is an open "o."   he caverns and groans engulfing: largerbonessoulsweddingrings

leaking from the socket of his anus: cocytus.   he stands apart involuntary.   pooped himself

false dreams it is often said take the entrance to this world for a home: how he is led
of course nobody loves him.   except the few who do.   broad spaces of voicelessness

kenny crossing on the ferry.   the ungenerous light of a moon hidden from view
he knows the way.   he trembles bracing: the hollow of his body delicately yields

[the thicknesses of victor decreased: blanket $\longrightarrow$ sheet $\longrightarrow$ floss. until no material would do]

the thicknesses of victor decreased: blanket $\longrightarrow$ sheet $\longrightarrow$ floss.   until no material would do

in the shedding season: the few of us who had not turned had found his remote room in mercy
he wriggled slight as a silkworm on its mulberry bed.   his lips spun slathering thread.   he sleaved

we waited for his release and he was released: yellow and radiant mariposa.   don't let us mend

[dead boys make the sweetest lovers. relationships unfold like stroke mags: tales less complex]

> . . . who could ever think—in particular, at this time, what gay man—that someone's death
> ever stopped the elaboration of someone else's fantasy about him?
> —D. A. Miller, *Bringing Out Barthes*

dead boys make the sweetest lovers.   relationships unfold like stroke mags: tales less complex
because they lack a certain tension.   several might be possessed and managed at once: properties
to be landed upon turn after turn: baltic ave.   st. james place.   time to roll those bones again

clean-cut jock in your treasure box: he is only ghost and polaroid.   your fist assumes his face:
the señor winces puppet trick.   his crack on the back so you can go both ways: brief resurrection

nudes prop themselves against the bed.   games evolve into storylines.   moments both pure and impure
the novel you write ends in many tragedies.   from which autobiography scarcely begins

[*tall and* thin *and young and lovely the* michael with kaposi's sarcoma *goes walking*]

tall and thin *and young and lovely the* michael with kaposi's sarcoma *goes walking*
and when he passes each one he passes goes "whisperwhisperwhisper."   star of beach blanket babylon

the sea washes his ankles with its white hair.   he sambas past the empty lifeguard tower
days like these who wouldn't swim at own risk: the horizon smiles like a karaoke drag queen
broad shoulders of surf shimmy forth as if to say "aw baby, sell it, sell it."   he's working again

towels lie farther apart.   the final stages: he can still do a dazzling turn *but each day*
smiles grow a little sharper.   he blames it on the bossanova.   he writes his own new arrangements

Tea Dance

Eleven Disco Songs That Equate Sex and Death
through an Elaborate Metaphor Called "Heaven":

1. "Paradise" [Change]

2. "Heaven Must Be Missing an Angel" [Tavares]

3. "Angel Eyes" [Lime]

4. "Heaven Must Have Sent You" [Bonnie Pointer]

5. "Take Me to Heaven" [Sylvester]

6. "So Close to Heaven" [Trix]

7. "Be with You" [Sylvester]

8. "Tripping on the Moon" [Cerrone]

9. "Earth Can Be Just Like Heaven" [The Weather Girls]

10. "Lift Off" [Patrick Cowley]

11. "Heaven's Where My Heart Is" [Marsha Raven]

—my personal "book of lists"

[heaven is a discotheque [*why don't you take me*] you could believe anything if you could believe]

heaven is a discotheque [*why don't you take me*]   you could believe anything if you could believe
god is conveniently present when we need to shake our fists at someone.   strike the tambourine

because you are a comicstrip version of your earthly self: cussing in maladicta balloons:
exaggerated in posture/in glide/in blurgits.   even the clouds feel like getting lucky with you
let alone all those hermes.   yours for the plucking: *lining up from side to side on sunset*

you have strobed moments of elegance: sipping for example whatever kickapoo joy juice is there
"3 x's" brand perhaps.   haloed in the light from the billiard room.   you torture each panel
with your fine looks.   the possibilities puzzle you: deeper into crosshatched corners

sundays go by the same as ever: funnies and glittery tea dances.   you still don't get the punchline

[now the mirrored rooms seem comic. shattered light: I once entered the world through dryice fog]

this was the season disco finally died
—Kevin Killian, *Bedrooms Have Windows*

now the mirrored rooms seem comic.   shattered light: I once entered the world through dryice fog
not quite fabulous.   just young and dumb and full.   come let me show you a sweep of constellations:

16, I was anybody's.   favorite song: *dance into my life* [donna summer]   and they did dance

17, first fake i.d.   I liked *walk away* [donna summer]   I ran with the big boys

18, by now I knew how to move.   on top of the speakers.   *give me a break* [vivien vee]

19, no one could touch me.   donna summer found god.   I didn't care.   *state of independence*

20, the year I went through the windshield.   sylvester sang *I want to be with you in heaven*
I said "you go" and "scared of you."   I listened to pamala stanley *I don't want to talk about it*

[the goodbye to nasty habits annual ball: scott smoking and drinking]

the goodbye to nasty habits annual ball: scott smoking and drinking
a new good riddance complete with that factory smell.   I wish them bluebirds

and o, how we danced on the night we divorced.   the ashtrays brimmed
bottles emptied into us: like thimbles to fill punchbowls.   and we sweated each other away

that was the morning of burnt out butts: dumpsters tall with those discarded abuses
the central nervous system cultivates a garden of tropisms about.   yes, it was a monday

who says that everything is explained in cycles.   work we once laid aside is taken up again
even the poorest taste has been developed: thirst defined by what quenches

a bad penny can be spent: on the useless.   or flattened by the weight of a moving train
to be taken out of circulation.   chain letter comes back unopened.   no: an invitation

[he'd make my bed jumble and squeak. a parrot must have lit inside. potty mouthed]

a song of Regan MacNeil

he'd make my bed jumble and squeak.   a parrot must have lit inside.   potty mouthed

I wouldn't have said, "quaquaquaquaqua" but his fingers pushed the dark: sores raised like letters

he wanted to gather all the air: buzzarding.   cold air flaps against the back of my skull

perched upon as a child bride: I felt my abdomen surge.   *captain howdy is kicking me*

hurt red pulp of a melon.   I bless the beak the tiny beak.   he has long black lashes like wings

[this is my last trick: if he has eyes they are escaping. the neighbors won't be able to describe]

a song of Sal Mineo

this is my last trick: if he has eyes they are escaping.   the neighbors won't be able to describe
when he flees his mane fans through the alley.   jerusalem palms beating against the doorway

in the blue hollywood hills behind the white hollywood sign where the falcons nest: I had lain
every letter shivered delighted under the swooping.   my feet drawn up into a careful vee

in the restroom at *the probe* I welcomed a sweet thrust.   pomegranate droplets dotted the commode

he was the disembodied voice of the planetarium.   I want to pretend it did not happen in the dark

[jackbooted. buttonflyed. hungering out of muni stations. spilling into clubs as sweet sweet tea]

a song of Patrick Cowley

jackbooted.   buttonflyed.   hungering out of muni stations.   spilling into clubs as sweet sweet tea
they chose me for a host: I was already carrying this choir in my head.   the language we share

the music had to magnify: silence would be unbear/unthinkable.   consider how sounds bodies make

now I lay me down these fierce tracks: bloodbeat & panting.   overtop an aspiration like release
music poured from me relentless.   no rest.   no rest.   a rapture bleating in the hills.   *going home*

joy for he whose song is done.   shirtless.   *before they say last call.*   I'm out among the multitude

[scott's at arm's length: I hold him at mirror distance. his pelt is familiar is my own skin]

scott at arm's length: I hold him at mirror distance.   his pelt is familiar is my own skin
my fingers undo him.   I wonder what I'll look like inside his flesh.   tight at latex as thing

our hands gather at our middle: a corsage.   a leather coin pouch.   the zipper's poking tongue
he is almost colorless.   I have faded things that suit him.   his face is my face but young

ruts already deepening between us.   cannot stand to watch.   we both make fists of our eyes
when I leave he is discarded chrysalis.   what have I become: [change] *I'll take you to paradise*

[and eventually I would take him back. into the reliquary of my mattress. winter terms]

and eventually I would take him back.   into the reliquary of my mattress.   winter terms
he stung like the briefest injection.   purples splotch inside the arms that were lifted by his grace

heaven can wait another hour for me.   I would use my teeth.   burn him with my whiskers

I spread him enormous and threadbare.   outside the world white as aspirin buries its hospital waste

my hands still clutch in an arc as large as his throat.   capillaries burst their deciduous branches

[between scott's asshole and his mouth I could not say which I preferred: perfect similes]

between scott's asshole and his mouth I could not say which I preferred: perfect similes
attention to cleanliness ran so deep.   I imagined a gleeming highway through the donner pass of him

a chill settling in his eyes: brown sierras.   I entered starving.   I could eat my weakest daughter

I want to hold a past larger than his shoes.   I want to say that summit closed its ribs around me
a story that omits resorts.   denies progress.   forgets how easily I traversed his altitudes

the truth: he was no monument.   sockets I plugged into.   warm circles I could make with my fingers
the truth: I have never left him.   I drive always toward california.   not all bodies recovered

[fifteen and smooth. light petting for a first ten smackers earned. budget inn. a man from napa]

> when I was ten, thirteen, twenty—I wanted candy, five dollars, a ride.
> —Essex Hemphill, *Ceremonies*

fifteen and smooth.   light petting for a first ten smackers earned.   budget inn.   a man from napa
we returned to the bar amid a dance of emergency lights.   one of many bodies I might have avoided

lips wrapped around his lifelessness: the swallow in mercy.   a throat unhinged to grouper size

[admission: I am a phag: afflicted with phagophagia]   seven times ruptured my esophagus:
1) betelnut. 2) greenglass. 3) pigbone. 4) spellingbook. 5) dressmakers' pins. 6) aspirin bottlecap. 7) comb.

and when I could afford to eat I ate away.   chewed hands off my ass.   chewed the saliva off tongues

[he must have been a deejay this one. the pulse quickens at another "lost companion" sale]

he must have been a deejay this one.   the pulse quickens at another "lost companion" sale
I filcher and dilber through crates of vinyl.   the glowing end of my glee cuffed in reverence

lovers carted away in stacks.   no needle to test them but I'm willing to take a chance
and the price is small.   any noise might easily be reduced: a matter of fading

the way the past is actively recaptured: not a whiff of poppers and halston z-14
no brief encounter with a surviving negative.   just a soundtrack undergoing reconstruction

he's a saint, he's a sinner   [the mix as a product of survival]   pushing up to 144 bpm

[your shiny buckle unfastens at last. we who were always tarnished and dingged up had marveled]

your shiny buckle unfastens at last.   we who were always tarnished and dingged up had marveled
certain tim was only gotten with soft hands no teeth and the patience that never tears xmas wrap

what a handsome package you made: an after-meal brusher.   an "always says please and thank you"
always I knew your polish would fade.   good child gone bad: a talkshow loomed with you on it

I didn't have to be right.   look I am loving you as you aren't: be even that bright square again

Spilling Tea

And when they got back to the kitchen, the cooks and helpers would ask the servers, "Well, did you spill the tea, girl?" Meaning, of course, was the gossip good?

—Billie Gordon, *You've Had Worse Things in Your Mouth*

[how would ed lower himself to sleep with her. an elaborate rigging of wheels and piano wire]

how would ed lower himself to sleep with her.   an elaborate rigging of wheels and piano wire
butching up for the role: "tell the katzenjammers to amscray."   he'd banish her barnes
or he'd swagger her out to the supper club: the perfect beard.   cupping her hand on his arm

& bob might never have known.   no latent signs: ed ogling skirts.   mounding potatoes like breasts
he didn't come home late & stanky.   smelling of imitation passion [by lez taylor] & warm kootchie

yes bob understood infidelity: elevated it to a high art.   a social circle ripe with peccadillos
but the strings were known and pulled with masterful care: punch & punch.   punch & no judy

[she was not expecting another gentleman caller. a golden male had already been brought forth]

she was not expecting another gentleman caller.   a golden male had already been brought forth
knuckles squeezed around the silver bedrail: she tried to wish a daughter out her womb

I was unwelcome mercury boy: swaddled in fever.   kindled & cracked like firebrand in the hearth
snatched still blazing from the fever I was salvaged.   o the double almost waste of a pansied room

a little girl was thrifted out of what had been discarded.   no natural sonny grime beneath my nails
I could only work the gentlest garden rows.   playing sous-chef, yarn-winder, pin-cushion, maid

mothers enjoy their forgery.   now the passion has cooled for my malleable act: a girlchild fails
I bury her ash daily.   smudged fingerprints: smoothing the soft mound within me where she stayed

[piano strings severed. papa the only record of your passions has been this gift of abscissions]

piano strings severed.   papa the only record of your passions has been this gift of abscissions
now I know you once had a voice buttermilk sweet.   hands: a pendulous udder waiting to be stroked

[how I've glued you together: retrieved under the family mercantile one ledger mismarked "dairy"]

farmboys smirked when you sang at the nazarene church.   discreetly they sent you bovine kisses
your ivory ticklers faltered.   cheeks swollen in presentation: forceful bulls entered from behind

[untitled]

when did the darkness climb on with its muscular legs pinning me under: goodnight uncle boo

giant teeth grazed me: he descended from the clouds.   wanting to explore the downthere of me

the biggest thumb.   I had to go bathroom but vines held me fast.   beanstalk sprouting my pyjamas

at the good of my trundle: magic beans could conjure him.   say it again: "I'll eat you up."

[a long line of bohunks and hunyaks: we settled in podunk. thirteen consonants]

a long line of bohunks and hunyaks: we settled in podunk.   thirteen consonants
surrounding a vowel with an umlaut.   that was the name we carried from ____tz____tz
into the new world.   in the grainbelt smackdab plopping down with our oxen and hogs

a cedar trunk in the junk-cluttered attic of a maiden aunt   [her name forgotten]
[so many ellipses in the tale of our begats]   keeper of tintypes.   christening gowns
the quilt patched out of hand-me-downs: scraps from grands and great-grands

difficult to say who we are in the present.   broadcast across farms like so many other seeds
threads of familiarity gradually unraveled.   whole generations apparently eaten by moths

[our family was tolerant of even anti-christs. but gramma had the recessive gene. now a lemon]

our family was tolerant of even anti-christs.   but gramma had the recessive gene.   now a lemon
the size of a lump grows in her bosom: she has bosom cancer.   *rock of ages cleft for me*

favoring jesus over her kith.   her kin ran away as soon as they mastered the knots of their laces
some never came home   [remember uncle clyde's last photo: a sailor's arm draping him like foxfur]

we are sad to be burying her so late in life.   with our own wicked money: casting pearls
her 86 years would buy back four flames I had to shovel over.   were death but a swapmeet

go on to glory kind stranger.   with our first stumbling steps we followed the heathens next door

[mornings sagged and creaked in bed: from the coalpit of our too small sleep I always rose first]

mornings sagged and creaked in bed: from the coalpit of our too small sleep I always rose first
meteors had struck and cooled in the concavity between us.   each day I left him swathed and still

lukewarm scott curled on his side: repository of my abortions.   distant systole muted by a pillow

night our undoing.   I tugged at the knot of his navel: breech blue crater where the sky fell in

[my sister-in-law never uttered his name. solving the problem of the open field: house sprawl]

my sister-in-law never uttered his name.   solving the problem of the open field: house sprawl
landscape reinforces the oldest edict: go forth and multiply.   subdivide.   amortize

my sister-in-law sends me an article: "it's okay to be single."   I have always been to her
resisting options to buy.   legal documents.   floor plans.   nothing down on an enclosed space

bound as I could be to another man: meadow surrounded us.   we were made safe by distances
in-laws became a town unvisited.   now the ground is broken.   but barrenness still can last

[what happened to "significant" out of bed: abolished in the act of standing. like a "lap"]

> They were regularly gay. They were gay every day.
> —Gertrude Stein, "Miss Furr and Miss Skeene"

your mom wanted you to get married.   she said.   and me standing right there.   her eye was fixing
beyond the shape of the neck you clung to at night.   we rubbed each other out: a pair of erasers

what happened to "significant" out of bed: abolished in the act of standing.   like a "lap"
otherwise we were only "others."   how significant could we remain even in vow

scenes from a wedding of two invisible men: roll after roll of over-developed film
all the world's mirrors won't have us.   at the cinemascopic margins: the eye must seek us

[who won't praise green. each minute to caress each minute blade of spring. green slice us open]

               a song of mayflies

who won't praise green.   each minute to caress each minute blade of spring.   green slice us open
spew of willow crotch: we float upward a whirling chaff.   sunlight sings in us *some glad morning*

when we are called we are called ephemera.   palpitating length of a psalm.   who isn't halfway gone
fatherless and childless: not a who will know us.   dazzled afternoon won't we widow ourselves away

Tea Rooms

Even in the grocery store or the laundromat, every time someone's eyes passed over me, holding me for a second, I felt a boost that sent me forward and made me capable of doing anything.

—A. M. Homes, "The 'I' of It"

[what direction will you take when the universe collapses. you who when you go must go someplace]

what direction will you take when the universe collapses.   you who when you go must go someplace
you who must have more to spend than the rest of your life: busfare for instance.   mileage coupons

you have lived with yourself these several long years and wasn't that enough.   the awe now worn
behind the vacations of which you are fond: a flinch of terror.   your loins sag in their hammock

once men gobbled the garbo of you.   no wonder reclusiveness: in the russian river of your veins
the salmon are murmuring.   you go to your bungalow.   you know your bungalow dark as a birthmark

[this little kiddie liked floors: he'd go bangbangbang with his head all day long. hammerhead tyke]

this little kiddie liked floors: he'd go bangbangbang with his head all day long.   hammerhead tyke
he wanted to penetrate the world à la cartoon rabbit.   the world took its pokes: "why I oughtta…"

nevermind the needling: born and raised in the briarpatch.   chiggerspitbullsuncle: how he got dug

baby butt back with that thickboned brain of his.   enough force could put a place soft and round

noggin againstfloor againstbedpost againstwindshield.   against the day 'sgotta give and cut deep

[the last dog of this boyishness is put to sleep. feckless fluffy pet: I am not saved fella]

the last dog of this boyishness is put to sleep.   feckless fluffy pet: I am not saved fella
a bully tore me: he who muffled your bark with his shoe.   your sternum cracked the house unguarded

I stray for us both.   when the shelters are full I skulk among bins.   under fire escapes

spanked.   owned.   fed.   I have been all that: I wag the hanky in my backpocket receptively

boy my runty prayers are with you.   my legs kick at night automatic.   we chase the squeaky ball
better this way: run pant.   I have been his bitch.   you'd recognize the smell on me as killing

[the daddy purrs. he is holding a leopard speedo. tonight he takes his sugar to tea]

the daddy purrs.   he is holding a leopard speedo.   tonight he takes his sugar to tea
"precioçilla" the pinguid man calls me.   "put it on" he says & I put it on.   "take it off"

I take it and take this piddling attention.   my manners may be vile.   I may drink from the saucer

to be kept at all is eiderdown: scruffy denizen of the alley.   he took me in a bent brass lamp

when I am old I will vanish like a genie.   my master's wishes granted: boypussy,boypussy,boypussy
someday my knuckles big as his and split.   I'll try picturing what I'll have done with my hands

[my neck a toothsome feeding ground. vespered swarms had drunk of me before this new batman]

a song of Robin

don't be fooled by costumes: I am still an orphan.   I move through his house by stealth.   I thieve
he won't last: when he kisses I'll pull away.   already I know the short attention span of my body

my neck a toothsome feeding ground.   vespered swarms had drunk of me before this new batman

down every dark corridor of gotham I seek my next guardian.   capes fly open: how hunger rushes

when I'm ready to be circled one will circle.   secret cave.   I can make his voice bounce back
boy wonder.   he will believe he is the one hero.   I must remember to wince when I feel his fangs

[I wore the green bandanna as often as I could. cheaper than planefare. less baggage]

> When you see a pretty boy with the slave auctioneer,
> the assumption is that he wants to be sold.
>   —Catullus

I wore the green bandanna as often as I could.   cheaper than planefare.   less baggage
back when I was meat & potatoes and no fruit I scored: polk salad.   a wallet of greens

a common condition of chickenhood: legs replicate the shape of a brittle pull-y bone.   [snap!]
already accustomed to intrusion I worked.   muscles relaxed from age 3 as I recollect: preverbal

how such a trade is chosen: espaliered to bend.   to inhabit a particular corner

guess I wanted that avenue leading me away.   the same spot in my heart where traffic stopped

[these moves were not acquired overnight. stop: extended palm. love: suggestion of a hug]

> waiting my time to be one of the supremes.
> —Walt Whitman, *Leaves of Grass*

these moves were not acquired overnight.   stop: extended palm.   love: suggestion of a hug
how many times did I learn to walk.   each new song an occasion of steps and turns
everyone saw that I was no ordinary canary.   talent scouts taloned me: chickenhawks

but mama said, "you can't hurry love, no"   what right did I have to assert these hips?

cheeks of putti blow me kisses from the cornice of a brownstone: partly the face is carved
and partly the wings insist.   I am not of this world.   I know others like me.   oh birdsong

[not even wanting to be the glamor puss: the chore in wardrobe. dressing an oversmoked voice]

a song of Julie London

not even wanting to be the glamor puss: the chore in wardrobe.   dressing an oversmoked voice
my sultry look wouldn't go 12 ways.   as in calendar girl.   as in a "girl can't help it" cameo

maybe I could reinvent the divorcee: the between-jack-and-bobby coquette.   slumming on la brea
if it could all be finale.   no jazz combo backing me into the limelight.   no rinse away hair

no burt reynolds luring me from retirement with plaintive air.   no cry me a fucking river

I could be happy in encino.   avoiding the reruns of me: nurse dixie mccall [always "stat"]
fretting over a crossword I could have already done classic.   an excess of bubkes might please

[only the cruisy toilets will suffer this rascal. mmm, darlings…your smiles taste like porcelain]

only the cruisy toilets will suffer this rascal.   mmm, darlings…your smiles taste like porcelain
have I told you lately blahblahblah oh no?   pity.   but I hear the curfew knell & so must bid adieu

you alone would believe in the fictive heart: scarified as you are with that shape it's given

no permanent fixture the flesh.   remember a match skating in a urinal.   I escape like a gasp

your names are unsummonable.   extinguished cigs.   I reach toward your ceiling.   dangled man

[the city is dying to be stylish. if only it meant more ugly shoes: a return to eye contact]

the city is dying to be stylish.   if only it meant more ugly shoes: a return to eye contact
"girl be sensible" we want to say to fashion victims [who become fashion vampires: no reflection]
they need to seem wan and bloodless.   trousers purchased sizes larger lend a pose of emaciation

in the windows of chichi stores dummies appear to be shrinking their waistlines: arriviste dummies
who's doing all this hair?   this lack of hair?   at the salon we flip through *oncology today*

some looks we look forward to looking back on.   remember ocean pacific.   remember angels' flights

[mannequins from the same lumber: correspondence of grains. perhaps the same grit finished us]

a song of Paul Cadmus's "Mannikins"

mannequins from the same lumber: correspondence of grains.   perhaps the same grit finished us
drawing us together.   sinistral hands overlapping the suggestion of genitalia.   we lack

no artist ever fills us in.   we sleep continent atop a history of unrequited pleasing

dumb showing.   we toy in earnest.   the attempt to conceal is also an attempt to divulge

[my stasis must confound you. if you have worshipped at all you must know what patience is required]

a song of Visconti's "Death in Venice"

my stasis must confound you.   if you have worshipped at all you must know what patience is required

see how the epicene tadzio trails behind the others: aware of your gaze and slightly bemused
you don't leave.   like that pitiful composer you're hooked.   yes you want to touch his hair

I must be fair now: the cobblestones are washed with bleach.   bedding smoulders in the piazza
irresistibility of endings: what if a flawless lad succumbs.   what if you catch your train on time

[rollingstock clatters through town and your cells urge to hop it. couplings of slatted cattlecars]

rollingstock clatters through town and your cells urge to hop it.   couplings of slatted cattlecars

the anatomy remembers where it came from: ~~||||~~.   shoulders hunch forward perpetually
the jab the belly anticipates.   out of habit eyes pull men in.   even the homely ones: ⊗

you could do a spread by rote.   [forgive the way the penis stirs at such a thought]
every inch of you courting ▭ .   rough and naff.   suppressing the gag response

a part of you will always pursue cars.   a suit of scars fitting to take that ride. ∞

[not just that you and I got starry-eyed—an epidemic of romances was sweeping around us. a falling]

not just that you and I got starry-eyed—an epidemic of romances was sweeping around us.   a falling

in "love in the time of caulifleur" [documentary of that age]   we're flanked by crowds of chemoheads
stalks of rappini towering in the public park: a sudden urgency grips each cruciferous vegetable

greensick in our salad days!   we cellophaned.   afraid of the rash our cravings would provoke
while the stench of toothy kisses wafted high.   in the streets we suspected passersby of sauerkraut

you were always firm to the touch: no signs of leafscorch or turnip blight.   rich in iron
and I picked at my plate: spat.   have the sidewalks wilted.   strike of the jealous sun

[elegy]

finally you are gone.   I began to think you the five brothers: each a different kind of indestructible

1) rugbaby, your mama hung you on the clothesline and worked you with a racket.   2) scalded you
3) were oopsed into a lake that spit you back.   4) intact your hard egg jigsawed a plate of glass

everyone [5] you included] took a crack.   you bounced back: ricochet biscuit?   *not this time, baby*
because the future cannot contain us: littleyou, littleme.   I drawing up the covers closed our eyes

Reading Tea

While on others thou art calling,
Do not pass me by

—Opening Hymn at Glide

[ode]

where have you gone blue middle of a decade?   the gates creak.   a sigh is so vastly different
the diary is pure spine.   in the most gingerly way each leaf opened reveals the less of you

83, 84, 85: your relics in a converse box.   adoring letters from one upon whom you put the kibosh
shade trees bent to listen for a song.   [erasure?]   all of your best composing is lament

faithless time you steal the handsome petals for yourself.   a bruised fist of hyacinth becomes you
when the wind bears no whisper but alack: an eye fears you & distance: the short distance across

[the crash divides my life. before I hadn't been known to fly: the simon magus secret]

the crash divides my life.   before I hadn't been known to fly: the simon magus secret
I believe we shattered the same bone on impact: left humerus.   godbless us where the scars knit

a spot of earth still tastes of me.   where starthistles gorged themselves.   ittybites, bittybites

soft shoulders kiss in the slump of night.   I still wake with infant vision.   egypt wrapped

one prefers "accident" over "destiny."   I set out from the dyingplace.   these presents are my feet
hadn't I had them before?   my hair the color of mud.   indentations where my body chose to give

[divining: where I come from is drought. nine years at a time so arid we worry each drop. dread]

divining: where I come from is drought.   nine years at a time so arid we worry each drop.   dread
ten-year flood.   generations named before and after rain.   two kinds of cracks two kinds of damage

decade of evaporation: I remember children light as tumbleweeds.   some were carried by the wind
some sunk deep into wells.   when I drink I am thirsting for those springs: captives of hard earth

this year I'll not see the lake at its capacity.   scarcely the hope of a postcard: dam view
so full one cannot find where trees abbreviated.   tantalizing faces on the surface and below

[intolerable phoenix: the prairie. I come lately to an expanse unbroken by the human form]

intolerable phoenix: the prairie.   I come lately to an expanse unbroken by the human form
grasses clew a bestial sphere: foxtail and turkeyfoot.   seeding with the plangency of fire

where are my vacant young tenements now?   I thought the terror of memory was its inescapability

goldenrod grows where it always has.   up as if from subways: bright thatch continually streaming
I have no tie to unplotted land: transient milkweed.   flocculent discharge borne ever more aloft

[the merit of reading tea: gunpowder variety unfurls puptent green. sleeping bags zipped together]

the merit of reading tea: gunpowder variety unfurls puptent green.   sleeping bags zipped together
all summer our mouths wore the parfûm of shattered blossoms.   see: you like butter your chin says

in a clearing in the wood we were made to play nice & dainty: petite cookies amid elegant service
were we taught to rub two sticks together?   proper steeping.   poise and balancing upon the knee

our leaftips turn silver.   one would wander in search of cress: strangling in the creekbed
each discovery triggered by a broken cup.   using a trusty fieldguide to earn badges: we identify

[how his body stood against a thicket. rich in hardwood gentry: ponderous and gloomy]

how his body stood against a thicket.   rich in hardwood gentry: ponderous and gloomy
the limbs would still extend a noble canopy had they not been so alluring: pitch and timber

hungry for plowland and pasture the notchers came.   char and rot the tools for clearing
driven deep into tangles the aching teams.   corduroy roads leading to the penetrable duff

he has been pioneered: given to the final stump allowing settlement.   slow collapse
these trees stripped and unable.   there was no child in him: a land traversed many times

signs dot the road where he should flourish.   could the sparse line on a sign indicate the forest

[sleek mechanical dart: the syringe noses into the blue vein marking the target of me]

sleek mechanical dart: the syringe noses into the blue vein marking the target of me
haven't I always looked away.   don't want to see what's inside me.   inside me or coming out
older than balder: older than I'd planned to be.   aliveness jars me.   what's sticking what sticks

in my dream the haruspex examines my entrails.   glyphs of the ancient chitterlings transcribed:
highballs. speedballs. chirujos. chickens. lues. spora. blasphemy. butter. bitters. epicac.
highrisk behavior posterchild: come reeve.   a thousand happy tourists in-&-out me.   I matterhorn

how much frivolity does the hypodermic draw away: does it taste men waferthin who blest my tongue
does it know knees I've dandled on.   I feel taken in: darts in the waist of a coat I'll bury in

for I have husbanded recklessly: wedding daggers.   holes in my memory of holes: danaidic vessels
the needle quivers.   sickens.   I spill names an alphabetsoup of hemoglobin.   someone cracks the code

in a fortnight of waiting I draw up a will.   develop false symptoms.   how will I survive surviving

I'll throw parties where death blindfolded is spun: won't someone be stuck.   and won't I be missed

[my back is not straight. I have cradled the precious crutched and crutchless. crippled streets]

a song of Glide Memorial Methodist Church

my back is not straight.   I have cradled the precious crutched and crutchless.   crippled streets
the weight of these voyagers sways me.   I make strong jaws with my arms to hold them: lump of salt

wholecloth mouth unfolding.   the shout rattles along my roof.   eruption: a splintered pequod
my joy is leviathan.   in the bay the buoys are clanging.   I rise from the deep: gullet faithful

their gladness spills out on the land: I open wide a sextant.   let them find their bearings and walk on

[epithalamion]

say amen somebody.   the pews are hickory-hard I'm sick of sitting.   sick of hazy secondhand god
I'm gawky and greedy.   full of longing like frankie in "a member of the wedding."   here comes andy
alabaster betrothed: his pierced wooden groom casts a doleful glance.   *his eye is on the sparrow*

they took my heart gave thanks and brake it.   they are wounded by love: I must taste such a kiss
andy is lifted by outstretched arms.   slanted starlight and twisted shade.   I'm no more afraid
secretly I've brought my valise: "they are the we of me."   together we'll *steal away steal away*

[first fugue]

sweet birds sang: *there is trouble in paradise today.*　and we sweated each other away:　shirtless
you and I afforded ourselves:　a land traversed many times.　nights of undoing
lover divine and perfect comrade.　*I always wanted someone like you.*　now the ground is braking

visitation is brief but exact.　smiles grow a little sharper.　no more expectations
ears in lips and no more wit.　*and I'm still real hot then you kiss me there.*　we toy in earnest
slow tyranny of moonlight:　dead boys make the sweetest lovers.　if they could all be　finale

they pass too quickly out of breath.　*I feel real when you touch me.*　the night is an open "o"
erased metropolis reassembled:　the anatomy remembers where it came from.　up as if from subways
reveries are rivers:　*why don't you take me to heaven?*　the shiny buckle unfastens　at last

Lunch

At last we had to let them speak, the children whom flowers had made statues
For the rivers of water which came from their funnel;
And we stood there in the middle of existence
Dazzled by the white paraffin of lunch.

—Kenneth Koch, "Lunch"

[second fugue]

a poisonal cup: they can tell that their little boy is lonesome which he is

lifting belly seeks pleasure: in this position.   of wishing between his thighs

I must say grace over his thighs.   if you know how to say *pansy* say *pansies*

certainly some said this of him.   you still can hear them: spreading a blanket

even the telling   [which might annoy them does annoy them]   alas a dirty word

and not *annoy*: *anoint*.   anneal this rude flesh with balm and aloes

lilies.   sorghum and sour apples barely keep him: lily wet lily wet while

one taste one tack, one taste one bottle.   an infant dose.   on the nightstand

no more doves can land here.   the pigeon on the grass alas and the magpie in the sky

expect to rest just as well.   a second coming: when this you see remember

Softly and Tenderly

I have been to lots of parties
and acted perfectly disgraceful
but I never actually collapsed
oh Lana Turner we love you get up
—Frank O'Hara, "Poem"

[of all the modern divisions: time splits]

of all the modern divisions: time splits
you are the one: lunch
egalitarian in your traverseability

more than embargoes or frontiers or zippers
can torture with visible boundaries
you invite [spreading a blanket] to be taken
kissed reverently upon the lips

may not always have you.   but we've had you
taken mementos.   hurried away to engage
a dull career.   meet you secretly.   on the side

[maybe he wears my trousers: lagniappe]

maybe he wears my trousers: lagniappe
he is the same age as my memory of him.   leaning
into the menial wage.   the pockets tattered

sorghum and sour apples barely keep him
bony: an architecture of tentposts.   supporting

constellations.   the points where light
enters: frayed patches.   weakening seams

[triptych]

once	we kissed	the world
goodbye	aware	that it
was dying	of all	contained
within	these lines	I'll keep
two breaths	and you	to one side
of me	laughing	on the nightstand

[studs and rings: favors of the piercing party]

> . . . and so he dug a hole deep in the ground,
> and went and whispered in it what kind of ears King Midas had.
> —Ovid

studs and rings: favors of the piercing party
hole in the head.   you got your rightwrongright ear
sent out in a press release: post self disclosure

boys admired your jewels.   for a time
you liked getting stuck.   and advertised

when did you close your legs: no openings
available you whisper like a tease.   but rumors
trail behind you in the reeds: "golden boy
has suggestive ears."   you still can hear them

—for Alec Anderson

[he pleasures me: a nasty flick. quiescent]

he pleasures me: a nasty flick.   quiescent
the still of him.   we set a long exposure

frame by frame: no candid voice over: the eye
so easily deceived requests a replay: how

many times the act can be performed
slo mo.   po mo.   ho mo.   iris into a field of blue

[slashed his foot as a boy. heel to toe]

slashed his foot as a boy.   heel to toe
on the living coral.   attempted to cure the sore
in a mortal swabbing: iodine

catalyst: pink branches of exo-skeleton
informed the soft canvas of limbs

mollusks were pried from his barrier.   feeding
frenzy of sharks at the jagged perimeter

polyps grown into a reef.   trawling ships
keep the distance.   he sings their sails away

[the mind is a shapely genital. faces: elaborate]

the mind is a shapely genital.   faces: elaborate
fig leaves.   disturbed by occasional gusts

modesty muh-dear.   admits impediment.   I don't
mind saying: like you better with your clothes
off.   but sober and with all your wits about

[personal]

HETERO LIFE WANTED: me to move in.   share
a double entendre.   2 fireplaces and a kid
spacious: a must see.   soon I'd be having my eggs

poached.   because that's the way I would like them
toast: cut to triangles.   napkins: folded to hats

but could we stand to grow up together.   learn
ABC's and respectable manners.   would I have to shake hands
with the guy pals: firm.   longing for the visegrip of thighs

[a conch: I washed ashore on more than one atoll]

a conch: I washed ashore on more than one atoll
no shipwrecked soul traced my steps.   archipelago
of private beaches.   I sought no rescue from maroon

yare sloops would nestle in my coves: come
to suck hermetic creatures from their shells.   girls
opened sweet blossoms for me: boys rubbed firm
nipples into my back.   buried me head in the sand

a youngster lashes himself to a raft.   classic
romance.   catches the drift: especially away

[my father and me making dresses: together]

my father and me making dresses: together
we debutantes.   cruel in lace bodices

we swoon to saxophones and rich husbands.   late
afternoon: shots of brandy in our cocoa

aren't I blessed with a young father firm
and flouncy: giggling in his petticoats

the other boys sigh when he mows the lawn
they fumble with their pockets and blush

while we two chums.   in a workshop of taffeta
never tire of chat: rugby or crushes or appliqué

I put my knee in his back.   I cinch and cinch
as preparing for an antebellum barbeque

where an ashley wilkes could be filled with regret
and atlanta explode its host of scarlet poppies

[my father and me in hollywood: fading and rising starlets]

my father and me in hollywood: fading and rising starlets
look at me as sandra dee.   and he: the drugstore lana turner

how life imitates "imitation of life."   we were of two minds

the actress and her actress daughter mirror the actress/daughter
dynamic of the father/son mother/daughter charade

I tweedled as dumb as sandra dee was.   and as sandra dum
doted on daddy I doted on daddy's boyfriend.   and daddy

that has-been with his porcelana skin creme and his mafioso
brought out the bitter lezzie in me.   oh: as in "we were white."

but he could have been the patient dark-skinned housekeeper
a cut above a mammy mommy dearest daddy.   and I
the bitchy high yellow ungrateful child who passed as easily
as white.   as I was a white black child actress anywho

at the end of my father.   the end of the hollywood star
at the end of the fifties.   at the end of beauty itself

I cast myself as myself on his/her casket while mahalia
jackson sang sweet swing low sweet cheryl crane
sandra dee daughter/son black & white technicolor refrains.   oh sweet
mommy/daddy oh poor porcelana turner I love you.   get up

—for Peter Gizzi

[my fingers have performed their services: church steeple people]

jo (Scottish): sweetheart (pl. joes)
JO (Queer): jack-off

my fingers have performed their services: church steeple people
all bald.   all slender: the chapped rafters where a prayer echoes

have congregated round me.   clamored to be baptized
in the name of some daddy.   some boy.   some holy ghost

I have allowed this decalogue dominion: census takers
who tally by heads.   cradle me stealthily as mary and st. jos.

[patron of families.   confectioners.   and funeral directors]
and take me after a passion: anneal this rude flesh with balm and aloes

I have counted upon their strokes to uncrypt the dead.   *supernature*
to shatter the snowy vessel [rosebud]   where the eye's light slows

these ten have been my lovers: callous.   constant and inconstant
in their bad disguises.   flicker of trick-or-treaters in my bedclothes

pinky to thumb I count their names: kevin, danny, cliff, ernie, kenny,,,,,
the jeffs close in to me.   the joes.   and [curving and bending] the joes

Sweet By and By

Think of him, the one you loved, on his knees, on his elbows, his face turned up to look back in yours, his mouth dark in his dark beard. He was smiling because of you.

—Allen Barnett, *The Body and Its Dangers*

[simple endings overlap: grief is interference]

simple endings overlap: grief is interference
we don't call dead air by the sound it makes
a scratching of monkey's paw disrupts stillness

life is a poor edit.   clip cut and paste

journal of caducity: no entry yet under "I"
too young to have amassed this catalogue.   obits
collected butterfly wings.   clippings of a summer lawn

[the sad part of living is eating and dying]

the sad part of living is eating and dying
our dialogue breaks off mid-sentence

the bill arrives as a eulogy: itemized
everyone swallows a breathmint.   repression

nevermind the cost: I'll pick up your tab
you got the cab.   these days green and folding

[sounding the depths: she slides into the bath]

sounding the depths: she slides into the bath
displacement: acres of her frame bob as tiny azores
promontory of a neck above the diluvian world

why the tendency to represent ship as woman: buoyant
she is born from the sea.   anemone in its element

civilizations ended one drop at a time.   she held them
under: lost continents.   eventually the floods must subside
land is sighted: a new atlantis?   yawning the whirlpool widens

—for "Mother" Press Fulcher

[attended by miracles. every man has two angels]

a song of the apocrypha

attended by miracles.   every man has two angels
on duty.   how the divisions of hell quarrel
in the world to come: who shall be cast out

a bewitched young man: christ rises again
circumcised in the cave.   an idol falls
his death demanded to order in the church

we must fear god: militant and lying
christ at play makes a dead boy speak.   what
rules are given for this purpose: to suffer

[sheet wrapped as a burnoose. about his head]

sheet wrapped as a burnoose.   about his head
tubes fill his mouth with opium: diversions

keep him occupied: a palestine whose defenses
are suppressed.   territory lost.   frail arms
impuissant: his sky is a rattling dry gourd

here is a man from a country without borders
anyone can cross over: share his bed.   lazaretto

[the agricultural application of burial]

the agricultural application of burial
you're laying the lawn: a poultice roots
into the gash you cut in the ground

kenny.   service here is terrible
no decent waiting upon: cold picnic
over your salad memorial.   gnawed bones

I want to peel back the grass like bandages
just as I lift these corners.   shaking crumbs

[your torso: enticing to insects. like me]

your torso: enticing to insects.   like me
they want to bug you.   bugger you.   cocoons
pupate in those buttocks of adobe: anthills

untimely your nectar draws me: bouquet
exchanged for a pinwheel.   the foiled sentinel
over the stone sayonara which brailles itself
as a curious welcome mat: you took it for a hat

webs are your veil: tumulus beetles the maids
scramble to catch those spikenards.   a demimonde
by whom you are compromised.   in this position
imagination might have wedded us.   to share

[remembering the taste of skin: dim prehistory of dives]

remembering the taste of skin: dim prehistory of dives

secretions of the body: spume and seawater
cells of the voluble tongue welcome old chums

rapture of the deep: lungs fill with oceania
rubber suit flops into the skiff.   fins in the water

[choose equal weights: berries and sugar]

a song of Alice B. Toklas

choose equal weights: berries and sugar
a someone with influence.   likely to judge
twelve hours of maceration: skim and boil

any devoted friend might cook dishes
other than sweet ones.   august insupportable
and blisteringly hot yields little

jelly is ardently desired: simplest
or quickest to make.   remove from flame
and cool.   lest its delicacy should sour

[the minotaur at supper: spare the noritake and the spode]

the minotaur at supper: spare the noritake and the spode
from these ungular hands.   goblet stems scattered at my hoofs

a spattering of color on my hide.   remnants of one youth
another impaled on my horns: I must say grace over his thighs
for there may be no path back to him.   the way is dim and twists

myself am halfboy.   am beauty and the end of same: a hungry thing
hunts me also: through which passageway do my nostrils sense blood
what aperture brings me air salted with cries of the ancient corrida

[darling can you kill me: with your mickeymouse pillows]

darling can you kill me: with your mickeymouse pillows
when I'm a meager man.   with your exhaust pipe and hose

could you put me out: when I'm a mite a splinter a grain
a tatter a snip a sliver a whit a tittle.   habited by pain

would you bop me on the noggin: with a two by four
the trifle of me pissing myself.   slobbering infantile: or

wheezing in an oxygen tent.   won't you shut off the tank
mightn't you disconnect the plug: give the cord a proper yank

when I lose the feeling in my legs.   when my hands won't grip
and I'm a thread a reed a wrack a ruin: of clap and flux and grippe

with your smack connections could you dose me.   as I start my decline
would you put a bullet through me.   angel: no light left that is mine

—for Sam Witt

[thinking the think that falls away: my soul he has no hours to waste]

thinking the think that falls away: my soul he has no hours to waste
but is wasting word.   wonderful sport in losing.   *sere* and *wear* and *dree*

why would I want time now?   as if enduring a ragtag second of the galaxy
paints me noble.   me who complains at the sough of his own heartbeat

me who speaks no tomorrow: fluent in today.   me who likes *visit* and hates *stay*
my dwindling soul he went like hotcakes: me a success in the fine scant way

[you're thin again handsome. in our last]

you're thin again handsome.   in our last
hour together I'll be dabbing gravy off
your lip: stuck out.   an infirmary stoop

how can anything perplex us more than words
the pause in which we chew: parapraxia
I feed you lines.   you're a poor actor now
flubbing the bit part.   indignant us both

I'll want better for you than institutional
lunch in white paper.   pee stained underwear
a brief brief career as the delicious romantic lead

Gather at the River

Mine is a world foregone though not yet ended,—
An imagined garden grey with sundered boughs
And broken branches, wistful and unmended,
And mist that is more constant than all vows.

—Hart Crane, "Postscript"

[always returning: holidays and burials. not every week]

always returning: holidays and burials.   not every week
has had its good friday.   except that lately latches
left unfastened for me.   biscuits rise in the piesafe
a dark suit smells less like mothballs: chrism

and condolences.   calendars come gaily from the florist
accounts receivable.   time and the supplier of easter
lilies: collusion.   we sit cozy in the parlor together
a cenotaph of cousinry.   unexpected guests do drop in

[not the treats of quince blossoms. in this rainy cycle the yards]

not the treats of quince blossoms.   in this rainy cycle the yards
are so much muck.   levees do not so much break as buckle

we would let the river baptize and afterward: so relieved of pressures
the earth could slide back into place: the houses slide back into houses
and the river a river perhaps: a change in its squiggle.   new foulard

we have been hit worse.   have let waters reserve the next county
as a chained hound.   a second coming.   but with so few human casualties
the boating became a lark.   it wash away, we say, all this business

so we scrap: this, the little knickknack we salvaged from the last great storm
a bauble floats up in the night: calls us from among the darkest rushes

[autumn set us heavily to task: unrooted the dahlias]

autumn set us heavily to task: unrooted the dahlias
lay wrapped in the cellar.   cider pressing time.   grain milling
time to pick persimmons.   time to fix the leaky hayloft

slaughtering time.   rendering time.   time to put up chokecherries
take the woolens from the cedar chest: britches mending time
rabbit hunting time.   tallow candle dipping time.   soap making time

count the butter and egg money.   count the diapers in the wash
time to split wood and clean the flue.   time that the pesky swallows
in the chimney took their leave.   molasses cooking time

kids sent to glean the fields at dusk.   yams laid out to cure
and the last huckleberries balljarred in the larder.   corn husking time
clay dull red in sunlight crumbling: abundant the harvest and the tithe

[splat in the oatmeal: granddaddy facedown]

splat in the oatmeal: granddaddy facedown
disappeared the way a prize hog we were fond of

grandma got closer to: jeez.   not another
tale of armageddon.   she would beat us
at games of scrabble: biblical words latched
onto the vernacular.   challenges and curses

sometimes a prayer escapes: we are more
and less religious.   heaven hasn't swallowed her
up.   despite all our wishing it were so

[here comes the welcome wagon with its]

here comes the welcome wagon with its
melting pot: theory of assimilation

courteous gesture in swiss fondue
beware: the somber bass informs
beneath the overture brassly cordial

here come the long-handled forks
crusts of bread.   and such

[women stitching apron corners together. *neighborly*]

women stitching apron corners together.   *neighborly*
meaning free to walk beneath each other's clotheslines

parataxis of paperdoll mommies conjoin
cotton seraphim: tending the reckling brood

no jam jar is sacrosanct: hungry cubs
kiss their milk from the closest teat.   laundry

makes no clean sepiment.   between dwellings.   only arches
to parade through when called by name.   or aroma: fondly

this handsewn host descends with a tug
to wipe a smeared passel of lips: rinse

confection into the washbasin.   and would flock greyed
against the sky: winged and ready to take flight

[the future rose: an a-frame on the cumberland]

the future rose: an a-frame on the cumberland
pioneer stock tapering off.   balanced inclinations

fists forgot their hammers.   forearms atrophied
the frontier lay flattened against the roadway
wild things curled up: everyone was licked

cyclone improvements: the barn would not be replaced
nor would accents.   dulled in gentility: weakling wind

[splitzville for ann and mark: the tourniquet]

splitzville for ann and mark: the tourniquet
is cut loose.   no more cuts nor love bumps
cords around the neck.   bungee dives off the bed

he wears that bandage on his ring finger:
another woman stuffed in his drawers like a sock
he pulls her out at night: pummels her face
with those big lips.   puts out his flashlight

dreams are tight things with breasts.   triplets
pinch his cheeks.   when he feints to plant
a kiss he wakes: mouth full of chewed on sheets

[he achieved his escape: john wesley]

he achieved his escape: john wesley
from the slow assault of hands.   plunged
off the trestle neck and spine
snapping of kettle-fried chicken bones

a tablecloth laid over his remains
these collard.   this grits
the succulent drumsticks bearing witness
in a gathering of dixie-battered hens

[orphans of career day: the choicest lives already]

orphans of career day: the choicest lives already
appropriated.   sweatshops and gruel are beckoning

chairs and desks disappear one by one.   needle lifted
off the phonograph: all positions have been filled
they go forth on blistered feet.   vulgar talk

still the remembered tempo of music measures each step
a piper seems sweet.   the beat of drums and a line to enlist

[down with the chickenbumps you came: kerplunk]

down with the chickenbumps you came: kerplunk
spunky cannot play today.   at home with a case of school
work.   nothing on but election returns and black and
white ennui.   canned beanywienies are brother's fave
not yours: o for some frozen sympathy: dreamsicles
all the icecream they say you'll get when you get

what you got from that sibling.   the one you don't know
how to play with anymore: he's playing smear tackle
in the vacant lot.   while you hate his toy soldiers
bending their heads practically off: he'll be home late
slugging you in your "hey, that's my sore arm"
how brothers are buttholes: you write your theme for class

[he imitates his wife: no young drop from the gap]

he imitates his wife: no young drop from the gap
of wishing between his thighs.   confiscating a dream
he kicks her out of bed: always stealing covers

couvade: a man receives congratulations of his friends
aping maternity: the spurious faucet of his chest
suckles plastic dolls.   a practice labor
quivers across his tummy.   contractions

rouse him in the night.   she can bear the pain
and bears away.   as if no more burden than his touch

[dearest perdition. your sweet peach kisses lost]

> If we manage to suppress the Oedipus complex and marriage,
> what would be left for us to tell?
> —Roland Barthes

dearest perdition.   your sweet peach kisses lost
their true asperity: echolalia.   we go drunk
through another rehearsal: one another's guests

and are not bellicose.   I don't seem oedipusblind
nor you medeamad: casesura is the classical text
book case.   taciturn: we hold each other's breath

[baby's on a pallet. in the screenporch you iron]

baby's on a pallet.   in the screenporch you iron
bluing and starching to temporary perfection: fabrication
this acreage stales you in its chestnuts.   termagant
you are beyond your dolly expectations: saddled

you have a man with the talent to ted manure.   ripening
bark and worm castings scatter about your feet: flinch
hard to make it away.   the soiled dukes of his hands:
slops of his meals: tugging of his husbandry at your hem

[sonnet]

a song of the cinema

morsels of my lifeswork: the story of a professional party hostess
I call this film "edge that can't know what I'm taking with me"
familiar and not shakespiliar.   think *eurythmics* think *newamericanwriting*

a nice mix of plights and music.   boomerang boy and disco dollies
I call this film "edge of a terrific current issue full of vice"
going to have witchdoctors in it.   evil barbies.   caymans and gators

written in an enjoyable present: continuous.   an unresolved work
I think I'll call it "edge literate and fresh and ugly."   and "suitable?"
most of the shooting to be done in okinawa, okeechobee and omaha

most of the shooting nightlit super8 and under extreme conditions
roll credits: I call this film "edge that can't imagine how, given the situation"
suppose I'll be shopping for boots or intoxicants.   props and settings

if you get my machine I'm on location: hazy hot humid.   the far reaches
not to live, mind you.   to wrap up "edge where headed the winging cranes"

[the rain deliberately falls: as an older boy's hand]

the rain deliberately falls: as an older boy's hand
would drop into my lap.   I did like the wet
let trickle against my soft: disturbingly
precious the way I caught it.   mouth stretched wide

now I rush to cover up.   even the telling
clouds: frightening.   I wear my slicker outside
don't want to catch my death: feel its grip

126

[old age keeps its reservation. nostalgia]

old age keeps its reservation.   nostalgia
is best thought to be past: lap trays
pop up startlingly.   familiar playgrounds

spoon: a blunt instrument.   purees
and porridges stir the weak.   recall
faltering vision seeks some recognizable form

we know a bib.   remember a tune
curse the mushy texture of dear friends

with *teeth* wedded to *sink*: as in "under the"
distinction softens into pablum.   dissolves

In the Middle of the Air

first we were darkness, then we were galaxies,
traveling too fast too far for me to call

throughout all that space goodbye
my twin my half
of the light, goodbye my little bit famous—

—Brenda Hillman, "Time Zone"

[we all carry signs of our obsessions]

we all carry signs of our obsessions
you your needletracks.   I my stretchmarks

no sleuth need rummage our files

I flatten my belly: a hamlet ballerina
o that this tutu of solid flesh.   melt

[third-world hunger strikes you. midtown bus]

a song of the virus

third-world hunger strikes you.   midtown bus
passion settles in the tenderloin.   ravenous

you thrive on the gaunt busboy: chops
respond pavlovian to the tinkling of poverty

your wallet can afford you.   some protection
an allowance to rut among the cheaper cuts
a scavenger: you feed off them.   skinny skinny legs

[in the new genesis: a part of his skeleton became me. shaped me]

in the new genesis: a part of his skeleton became me.   shaped me
me as womb trembles forth.   me wifeless with 300,000 retro sons
me of no husband girdled and they to no spouse parceled: bits of gopherwood

theogony: must my skull be hut for them all?   at night the anvils sing *bingbong*
them kids is pounding out more kids.   listen: dna clinks its chainmail
old soldier my body cannot hold: rickety ark.   no more doves can land here

[you don't have syphilis. the doctor says]

you don't have syphilis.   the doctor says
you don't have hepatitis.   he says
you aren't diabetic.   the doctor says

cholesterol level normal.   blood pressure
good.   he says you've got great reflexes
the doctor says these things.   he's the doctor

he says I *do* have a bit of bad news.   he says
just like that: I *do* have a bit of bad news
not a *real* doctor remember: a physician's *assistant*

[because as lives are aching I am lucky: a poisonal cup]

because as lives are aching I am lucky: a poisonal cup
I ingest pill after mastodon pill.   after I have abdominal pains
headaches, skin aches, bone aches, the drowse and nausea

no matter pill or bitter pill.   but no milk rare and no meat fat
nor oysters: doctor's orders.   my mouth going blind over and over
nothing spicy or sharp.   forgetting I eat my hair.   I say our dear lord:

losing myself in public.   seems sunday loves my mouth and music
we supper [me and poison].   together we bath [poison and me].
we live together difficulty.   and fairly normal: doing all the poisoning myself

myself.   need no wine to sanctify.   as of the right now I am lucky:
need no litter bearer.   children undigested I am able to throw back up

[in the course of travel: strychnine every few hours. some italian art]

in the course of travel: strychnine every few hours.   some italian art
and trees yes pretty but it's the normal routine.   well, "normal routine"

you easterners: your maple trees.   you have your maple trees.   your nation
and me my eyes bugging late and funny: scrub compared to the maple trees

every few hours flash fevers.   every few and I'd be small.   a bit nervous
the evening distended as a pad patella: oh my knee.   and I had to pee

virtually every few minutes.   someone catches me under the maple trees
taken out of context: like a trip on a yacht or dying.com.   I would not go

there: among the trees I stood almost grand and well.   with my own nuts
my own birdlike nuts.   my own startled happiness at the slightest breeze

—for Tom Thompson

[when dementia begins: almost makes sense like hamburger translations]

when dementia begins: almost makes sense like hamburger translations
or the poems the body writes in its dysentery: explosions at either end and vile

my mind has many homes these days.   I have seen much of kitchen tile
much of the great round bowls.   in doorways I lose the heartbeat of decisions

me is no comfort place to be these days.   hang teeth and smiles in the windows
and fiddle fiddle with the thermostat.   but the mind don't stay: away to the mall

let the lookylous look: *rupt rush re so re bo re we re wa re yo reat reali reall*
see streets of a lost city.   the lights beyond keep blinking *how yet how yet hows*

[cherry elixir: the first medication. so mary poppins]

cherry elixir: the first medication.   so mary poppins
a chance to acclimate: an infant dose.   a baby step
supplanting pneumonia half a teaspoon at a time

until the tablet can be tolerated.   with adult strength
my throat constricts around unspeckled eggs: rosy boa

everybody talks about the cocktail: sounds delicious
I think in jello flavors.   picturing umbrellas in tall glass
the cocktail up.   the cocktail over.   straws and serviettes

not a steel spansule.   not a fistful of bloated tictacs.   no burn
in the bowels the belly & the mouth.   want my goddamn cocktail

Cocktails

. . . all the very gay places,
those 'come what may' places
where one relaxes on the axis of the wheel of life
to get the feel of life:
jazz and cocktails.

—Billy Strayhorn, "Lush Life"

Mixology

Ho! stand to your glasses steady!
'Tis all we have left to prize.
A cup to the dead already,—
Hurrah for the next that dies!

—Bartholomew Dowling, "The Revel: Time of the Famine and Plague in India"

[the cocktail hour finally arrives: whether ending a day at the office]

the cocktail hour finally arrives: whether ending a day at the office
or opening the orifice at 6am [legal again to pour in californica]: the time is always right

we need a little glamour and glamour arrives: plenty of chipped ice
a green jurassic palm tree planted.   a yellow spastic monkey swinging

a pink classic flamingo impaled upon the exuberant red of cherries
dash of bitters.   vermouth sweet.   enough rye whiskey to kill

this longing: I take my drinks stiff and stuffed with plastic.   like my lovers
my billfold full of rubbers.   **OPEN**s my mouth: its tiny neon lounge

[this is what you love: more people. you remember]

this is what you love: more people.   you remember
to say "of all the men I know" and "your nice friend kimber"

but it wasn't always so.   living in a big shoe and knotslips
in your bed the size of taxes [or texas?   you don't read lips

as well you should]   some hearing loss due to family
in your ears: homilies and hominy and decidedly no harmony

no wonder *the bad seed* topped your list of favorite flicks
having that brood crush you down into the mattress: you kicked

one fell out and the other nine said "rollover, rollover"
who could go to sleep with the sound of music?   and the hot covers

now you only regret men unbedded.   unwedded to your cheek-y
desire to lift strangers from taxis.   or texas: why be picky?

but you've gone "gee" in your ratings: shirley temple and madeline
volunteer work.   neighborhood meetings.   you even bring the gelatine

[he would care for me as a stranger: courtesy clerk. so quick]

he would care for me as a stranger: courtesy clerk.   so quick
that I scarcely noticed how he handled.   my eggs.   tomatoes
household explodeables.   each within its own white skin
the safeway around.   parts of bodies kept from rubbing
into cheese.   bleeding into delicate figs.   time was I was

a nasty little bugger: took a bite of every grocery clerk
and put them all back.   rosy cheeks faced out: hiding
what I'd done to make them rotten: I could not see
a clump of grapes and not think "pesticide."   crossing items

off my list I'd drift through the frozen aisle to piped-in
air supply: *all out of love*.   all out of häagen-dazs.   unmoved
by the way he called me angel biscuits.   hostess cake
as he tucked a receipt for my muskmelon into my jeans

[writing for a young man on the redline train: "to his boy mistress"]

> All the bodies we cannot touch
> are like harps. Toucht by the mind
> > —Robert Duncan, "Fragments of a Disordered Devotion"

writing for a young man on the redline train: "to his boy mistress"
first to praise his frame: pliable as hickory.   his greasy locks waxy ears
I'll stop the world and melt with you brustling through a nearby headset

if I had time to ride this monster to the end I would: hung by handstraps
jostle through the downtown stations.   each stop bringing us closer
to what? gether?   perhaps: or that exit of the tunnel where I look back

and *poof:* no lover.   men have led shameful lives for less proportioned fare
tossing greetings thick as rapunzel's hair: "anybody ever told you that you
[ugh, here it comes lads, stifle those chortles] resemble a young james dean?"

why *fiddle-dee-dee,* he bats his lids: the fantasy already turning to ruin
what if he debarked at my destination of pure coincidence?   followed
through the coppice of the square: fox and hound, fox and hound

I'd lead him on a merry chase: pausing every few: admire a fedora
check the windows of the haberdashers and cruise the sartorial shops
until I felt his winded breathing on my neck: yawned and departed again

we could while away the afternoon just so.   but at my back, etc

fresh and sprouting in chestnut-colored pubes is how I'd want him
not after the dregs of cigarettes.   the years of too many scotch sours
why, I wouldn't even know what to say to one who drinks scotch sours

except, "sir."   and "tough luck about those redsox" [which it always is]
now I've spent myself in lines and lost.   where is that boy of yesteryear?
let him die young and leave a pretty corpse: die with his legs in the air

[in the elegant days of downtown: we sunned on the porch]

in the elegant days of downtown: we sunned on the porch
no nose cancers grew.   no deep lines in our brows.   we lived

with a gassy dog.   tempestive guests.   a lawyer for a slumlord
a counselor next door and a trashman next door to that

the couch smelled where rotten pears had melted in the cushions
the coffee tasted burnt.   the whole house wept: a martini glass

was it the staircase that groaned?   boards under the carpet
that swamp cooler or the door that came unhinged at a touch

was it the picture of jesus over the mantel or the aceldama drops
from the red wax of the candles in their tarnished candelabras

iceblocks deliquescing in the kitchen.   pipes gargling the commode
that dog breaking wind in his sleep with the *hooty hoot* of a barn owl

perhaps someone's trick liquored up: stinking with navy stories
until we conked him.   rolled him down the steps in a drum

abundant as grass the graces touched us.   leaching through the walls
humming through oscillations of the sundering aluminum fans

in the wee light: a wilding song unsettled.   a bell for the coming mass

[gardenhose dilated with rain: a puff adder]

> . . . when the water receded it left depressions shaped like graves in orchards.
> —Tracy Kidder, *The Road to Yuba City: A Journey into the Juan Corona Murders*

gardenhose dilated with rain: a puff adder
so we retreat like tigers.   tails between our legs

summer: so crazy about peaches we're crazy
driving through orchards and the brown silt
clings to us.   flesh clings to pit: our hearts are woody

twenty-six bruised males planted face up
under the supplicant branches.   honey stench
something wormed hard into their boyish clefts

"when I was a tortilla salesman," I'm apt to begin
in the hum of pigs' blood and the sigh of cottonwood of

braceros with bedroom smiles and bad teeth who tooled
their names into their leather belts with the blunt tip
of a machete.   who harrowed bindweed and ragwort

and dropped their dungarees behind the flats of freestone
¿como?   how the eye drips with *corona* and prayers
mumble skyward: crows instead of kisses, *amigo*

[*amigo, n.*—friend, familiar, or an interjection like "halt"]

149

I too made love to *nameless male no. 17:* his hair curled around
his dagger tattoo suspended over his heart.   he said:

and I answered in the same tongue.   seedling
your roots exposed along with a chambray shirt: tugging
you out of the earth: naked.   trampled.   pulp.   scythe

I called you darling 14 ways.   I called you *peaches*

[winter moon summer moon budding moon barley moon]

a song of almanacs

winter moon summer moon budding moon barley moon
moon when the leaves are green.   moon when horns break off
the kindly moon the cooking moon moons for famine: big and little

a moon for raccoons a moon for the trees to pop.   chaste moon
the moon that makes eyes sore from the bright of snow
a moon sassafras a moon of ice a moon for awakening: a peach

moon of the terrible moon disputed.   returning geese scattered in formation
the oak the peony long night the storm the moon in the middle of summer
a trap a bone a hungry ghost   m [∞] n   the lightning the ripening berries

[a happiest harbinger to you: here spring]

a happiest harbinger to you: here spring
has a crocus to send out.   which is the parade
and hog day and cogitating bulbs in the temple of ground

your body is everywhere this fine day: a downy hare
a slender magnolia bud.   the whistle in pussywillow
in sanfrancisco the chinese and dragons hoot.   all about

scott: the easter of my astrological garden.   cherry blossom
pink and a hummingbird sprung from blue.   splinter
you're scott on limbs naked blooming.   spread your living arms

[chapt. ex ex ex eye vee: in which scott has a birthday]

chapt. ex ex ex eye vee: in which scott has a birthday
[*many happy returns of the day,* says piglet] & buys himself a puppy

soon the scent of burning leaves is too much.   hunting season
the crisp flannel air and hot oatmeal: instead of fishin'

crunching out through the yawping woods.   with his terrier
legs spindled as muskets.   his slight chest heaves.   his slender derriere

a pale chalkmark among the birches.   for a time he sits and smokes
scratching the curious brown dog behind its ears.   then snow

dusting down like dandruff on their collars.   they wait on haunches
listen for the woodchuck or roebuck: they have their lunches

and the whiteness covers them almost completely.   almost
far enough away from this moon and those rabbits and the geese

[dogs and boys can treat you like trash. and dogs do love trash]

dogs and boys can treat you like trash.   and dogs do love trash
to nuzzle their muzzles.   they slather with tongues that smell like their nuts

but the boys are fickle when they lick you.   they stick you with twigs
and roll you over like roaches.   then off with another: those sluts

with their asses so tight you couldn't get them to budge for a turd
so unlike the dogs: who will turn in a circle showing & showing their butts

a dog on a leash: a friend in the world.   he'll crawl into bed on all fours
and curl up at your toes.   he'll give you his nose.   he'll slobber on cuts

a dog is not fragile; he's fixed.   but a boy: cannot give you his love
he closes his eyes to your kisses.   he hisses.   a boy is a putz

with a sponge for a brain.   and a mop for a heart: he'll soak up your love
if you let him and leave you as dry as a cork.   he'll punch out your guts

when a boy goes away: to another boy's arms.   what else can you do
but lie down with the dogs.   with the hounds with the curs.   with the mutts

[12-line poem, seemingly out of place]

a bad translation of Pushkin, ending with a line from a John Waters movie

then the vehicular manslaughter took place: a tornado
of metal and suffering in the crosswalk: my god
he must have lost consciousness there where two marys
with very different handbags stood working

these days the block has its crossing guard: the mayor
sends volunteers in hats and sashes: to guard what?
can this bloodstained place be carjacked, eaten by rats?
will the dead like giants invade folks' imaginations?

or will the past reverse itself: a speeding ferrari
so that no lean body lies broken in the intersection
so that poor bastard isn't missed.   isn't starved after
by ladies, boys, wretches who holler *eggs, eggs, eggs*

[the mind of moss: sitting here by the reflecting pool]

the mind of moss: sitting here by the reflecting pool
hoping our shapes will never change.   as if

attention to form will save us from foundering
from cold cereal.   and from serious young men

who could forgive our weakening loyalties

water doesn't hold our place: one day
we set down the long russian novel we've been ~~living~~ [writing?]

and the names of the characters blur.   the plot
becomes completely twisted: the way we once forgot

the names of the 7 dwarves.   also the dog's birthday also
a luncheon with kind aunt sarah.   and when we return

a child has folded the pages into paper sailboats
look: little rudderless skiffs listing and drifting

time to abandon this silly regatta.   time to skip stones

[when you touch down upon this earth. little reindeers]

when you touch down upon this earth.   little reindeers
hoofing murderously at the gray slate roof: I lie beneath
dearest father xmas: will you bring me another 17 years

you gave me my first tin star and my first tin wreath
warm socks tangerines and a sloppy midnight kiss
I left you tollhouse cookies.   you left me bloody briefs

lipodystrophy neurosthesia neutropenia mild psychosis
increased liver enzymes increased bilirubin and a sweater
don't get me wrong: I like the sweater.   though it itches

but what's the use of being pretty if I won't get better?
bouncing me against your red woolies you whisper: *dear
boy:* unzip your enormous sack.   pull me quick into winter

[this little treatment has side effects: side effects]

this little treatment has side effects: side effects
including [but not limited to] poseidon emerging from the sea
striking his patinaed trident against the shore of my muscle
beach party: tremulant.   a quake.   a tension and slack in the arches

or the seawall inside me breaks: torrents.   did I mention horses?
they whinny snort and neigh up my pipes: herd music
and the squall that rocks my dandy timbers.   snaps my mizzen

the tablet I accept as a gift from god.   must be crushed
absorbed without food.   in this way it is like faith: senseless
yet entirely restorative.   mind you: the urge to crap is immediate

the black and red pill comforts me.   the yellow one
[I have to think: was that the one for sharon tate
in *valley of the dolls?*] induces dreams: I am hecuba
achilles.   three ugly fates in combination: spin measure cut

[*hope you like this new doctor*: rachel says in hopeful tones]

hope you like this new doctor: rachel says in hopeful tones
and I: *too early to tell.*   though hope does hover in my chest

certainly I've abandoned miss america-sized wishes:
world peace?   an end to hunger?   not while we consume, consume

I make hope the size of a bar of soap: hope-on-a-rope
like "hope there's not a spider in the shower this morning"

"hope some broadway producer brings back *starlight express*"
"maybe figs will be available fresh for a longer season

[without the global warming, I should add, in case god listens]"
and "maybe sheila e. will release a disc as good as *the glamorous life*"

my pulse drums too: a scant crew of leukocytes raise their tiny oars
these few who have not mutinied.   I want to lift their spirits

as we're crossing the equator: showered with a fine warm mist
I sing them a dusty springfield song.   soon the cabin's steamy

and we're *wishin' and hopin'* like there's no tomorrow.   but there *is*
already dawn: the passage safe: the mermaids beckon from the cape

                                                    —*for Rachel Zucker*

[my lover my phlebotomist. his elastic fingers encircle my arm]

my lover my phlebotomist.   his elastic fingers encircle my arm
psychopompos: he guides me away from my worldly woes.   his prick
cutaneous ——▶ subcutaneous ——▶ intravenous.   an underground passageway

I rise to meet him: engorged.   I wear a negligee and surgical mask
he's fat with smalltalk: "this fog" he says.   and "keeping busy?"   I am
I say "sometimes seems like all you want is blood."   he's sheepish today

maybe he wants to hold me to his brutal chest.   wrap me in gauze
press his coffee breath into my mouth.   our tongues: snakes: caduceus
then quickly the affair is over.   out on the street: my feet are swinging

my bloody valentine.   *sweet comic valentine.*

stay

. . . .

Filmography

If we go to the movies often enough and in a sufficiently reverent spirit, they will become more absorbing than the outer world, and the problems of reality will cease to burden us.

—Quentin Crisp

[robe and pajamas, steadfast and softer than anyone who touched me]

Papa's Delicate Condition (1963, George Marshall, dir.)

robe and pajamas, steadfast and softer than anyone who touched me

in the blear night dark: black your spine a musty bible.   we sway together

wrinkled lovers with tousled hair—a cocktail in hand—a pillow drenched in sweat

snowdrifts of terrycloth soaking where I spilled—mostly water: we measure
in drams and centiliters and shots: give me another, my sotted boys.   *roll footage:*

A LIFETIME OF HAPPINESS CONDENSED.   or, HAPPINESS OF A LIFETIME CONDENSED
we slip and slop and spill our soup—we pop our rocks—droop and droplet
flung over the back of the sofa: limp as a cashmere coverlet.   damp as a bloodclot

takes after his *(insert member here)* I heard of others.   but me?   I took after the dog

I don't know who brought these strawberry gin blossoms but surely they are mine
won't they look lovely next to the tv—the vd—the pictures of mom and pop

who fell in love with the circus.   brought it home every night: we cleared
beer bottles off the endtables: there, the stinko bears had room to dance their dance

[a mule-drawn scraper packed this earth: levees]

Ode to Billy Joe (1976, Max Baer, Jr., dir.)

a mule-drawn scraper packed this earth: levees
mounded into ossuaries.   many a first flower
enjoyed the mud and let itself be plucked away
from church picnics.   the gathering of men in fields

"what do you remember about the first?"
"I remember the lids of his eyes.   the cup of his hand
under my head in the tall grass.   a sharp pain
in my guts: I remember saying the words:"

branching from the main body of the river
sumptuous sloughs and overflows: dissipating
potential floods.   neither depth nor velocity is attained

under the bridge.   half out of the moon.   overalls
bunched around our ankles.   a shame of a kiss
I cannot stay here: the river opens and swallows me

suppose the trawlers & dredgers continued the search
certain I had gone under a log: pinned.   the steady current
hounds sniffed under brush to catch my scent

miles downstream: lanterns swung out over the water
dreaming of my face.   the faces I had dreamt arose
on the roads: the coats of watchers.   uncloaking the new life

save those foxgloves pressed in the empty pages of genealogy
I lost the way back on purpose.   the delta empties into the sea

[19 lines]

Looking for Mr. G   bar (1977, Richard Brooks, dir.)

shapes repeat themselves.   and messages rewind
it's the answering machine you don't want to hear from

"I could never be kept," he says.   the fear of sobriety
wets his tongue: slips it into my ear with his number

sitting in prospect park bar: conveniently contained
by the lack of scenery.   his shorts creep up his leg

hand: too casual.   considering his inner thigh
parts of the same body arouse each other: kissing cousins

we all sleep with men who are not our lovers: economically
the barter is proposed: more drinks on the mastercard

the pitch and roll of a bed crosses my mind.   how to end
this groping beneath the formica table: nobody walks away

I used to wake beside the same body for years
its contours familiar: until it no longer suited

who knows where desire goes when it leaves the bed
a stranger comes to sit with me: we both light up

he's had a lover test positive.   his lips find my neck
his hand, his ass: I consider the risk of each part I want

there is a covert exit.   a cab waiting.   I sign for us both

[I was a priapic boy: the prow of a galleon]

Hook (1991, Steven Spielberg, dir.)

I was a priapic boy: the prow of a galleon
breaking through the warm caribée.   *avast*

the babysitter and I playing hide and seek
no search party: just him wrestling against me:

chained to the armoire.   a belt in my mouth
my knobby prisoner embouchured by his breathing hole

I was always a lost boy: swept into the nevernever
one among the private order.   who hung out

long after dark.   caught lightning bugs.   who
erected forts: buttressed against quizzical adulthood

who were hairless and soprano and angelically ungendered
whose dirtiest word was *balls:* those things we lacked

a strange kid would yank our underwear up our cracks
he and his nasty friends hid by the creek and smoked

"mama wants to know what's happened to your shirt
how come you come home without it?"

he said I had pretty hands.   as he tied them to the dresser

I was the boy who dreamed he could fly

I do believe   [clap your hands]   I do believe

[a boy at 15 can't be too tough: approximate masculinity]

My Own Private Idaho (1991, Gus Van Sant, dir.)

a boy at 15 can't be too tough: approximate masculinity
holds the daisy of his features clenched: raw and slight
a pebble of a rump.   scrawny his penis a plucked sparrow

his one talent: the ease of ejaculate.   not as handy as french

autos pass.   he shudders: imagines your bullet lodged

spiss and spiff: the way a hefty bag can contain him
along the highways speckles dot the grass.   is it easter?
he had that basket.   those lovely golden eggs

he had that blue-veined oyster you could cut with a knife

you had that *I'll take you as far as you dare* kind of look

when you pulled over: swirl of dust.   rubbish in safety orange

[every man needs a buddy. who'll do]

Making Love (1982, Arthur Hiller, dir.)

every man needs a buddy.   who'll do
when the wife has gone to the in-laws

the evening had already lowered.   he crossed
his legs in the manly way: outside

kids who could have been his yelled
"you're out."   and "no sir!"

eddie's two-bit country-singer looks: not my usual
dish of icecream.   and since he's mom's best friend's
live-in's daughter's hubbie.   the danger quickens

in the shed behind the natatorium: everyone knows
the device.   a meeting with the gardener's son

his voice rises and trembles: a steel guitar
the song of inalimental marriage.   he slobbers

on that part of me that is not woman.   his throat
an undergarment: silky and inviting

"man o man o god o man"   no confusion
about gender.   or the home he boomerangs to:
the good *she* who holds his place at supper

a man returns to his wife.   I understand the geometry
this is no equilateral triangle: compliments are exchanged

featherriver honkytonk: in the backrow I wait
so any life elapses under just such conditions:

no holidays.   no home.   relegated to odd nights
the frontseat of his car in lieu of the conjugal bed

he will never take his boots off

    *　*　*　*

"the act," he says.   meaning his career

[college roommate gone: his hamper full. I'll do us both a favor]

My Beautiful Launderette (1985, Stephen Frears, dir.)

college roommate gone: his hamper full.   I'll do us both a favor
sorting his socks like demented wife.   smoothing the pillowcase
its callipygous dent splayed bonewhite: spluttered where I laid him

what is a friend but a lover held at bay?   we find our quarry
want to tear each other: canines exposed.   our leashes tangle
grant us the safety of fenced-in yards: we worry the neighbors

love is seldom a dull chore: I know how to fold his t-shirts
how they smell before and after.   washing and tumbling
piggish delight the rooting after truffles.   whiff and snout

in his absence I build a model of him.   clothed in white undies
starched where he's starched and softened where he's soft
I use his favorite bounce.   bleach-free tide to hinder chafing

in separate rooms we count on our fingers the passing hours
we know the way each door swings open: how to find each other
agitating in the dark: sheets snaps elastic and those clumsy buttons

[the man in the front row: uniformed. ugly as my father the disillusioned]

Nashville (1975, Robert Altman, dir.)

the man in the front row: uniformed.   ugly as my father the disillusioned
train tracks ripped from the ridge.   fireworks over point charlie in his brain:

last night the barn swallows called me to the home place, he said.   I reckon he sleeps
in spangled drills and fire batons.   and in between a kind of peace: whippoorwills

there I sat and heard the call from the linseed-oiled perch of the choir: that was before
soldier pants parted the wings of their crotches or bluejays stole my trinkets

fiddles   grey geese   gingham   chokecherry jam   gnarled bark of a slippery elm

hills that knew us as they knew sunlight and the crash of hickory branches falling

now factories and country inns.   amusement parks.   dilapidated monuments
old ada on a respirator.   erma crazy.   tolbert weekending at the chicken farm

where we grew lanky and religious.   praised ammo and passed the lima beans
longing for dresden or paris (tennessee).   the far parthenon on a back lot in nashville

not this tarpaper hut in the holler where I was christened: *varmint* and *tater pie*
someone once said I called to mind a character in *snuffy smith.   god's little acre*

yes, it was just like that: bacon rind, wood stove, dynamite.   uncle burr kicked by mule
papa with a cottonmouth.   roe and ray in the pokey.   the night the kids got kerosene . . .

and: the last time I was in those hills I burned with fever.   drank water from an old jar
prayed in a tent in the woods until I felt the spirit leave me: in darkness, in utter dark

I can't imagine anymore.   dead hawk hung on the fence: fledglings in the snow
the rustle of some marcescent blossom: louisiana hayride, grand ole opry, WTNV

white lightning, daddykins, cemetery: *life may be a one-way street, but it don't worry me*

[morning broke on my cabin inverted. tempest in my forehead]

The Poseidon Adventure (1972, Ronald Neame, dir.)

morning broke on my cabin inverted.   tempest in my forehead
a fine kettle of fish, I'd tell myself, could I have pinpointed the date

marked SERO-CONVERSION in my pocket gregorian calendar.   [a guess?
sometime between the day lady day died and the day lady di died]

my lymphocyte is no gillyflower.   respiration no nightingale trilling in the dark
to those who hear crickets in sputum and the nightwind rasping in breath

I say: there is no positivity in being positive.   all that glitters is glitter

and so we have. . . .   the climb:

first, think of all that can be jettisoned.   cumbersome clothes for example
[always the one thing I'd think of doing without]   when I was young

in borrowed 501s: had to have pants so someone could want to get in them
without boxers for weeks I could make do.   not beyond wearing slinky panties

if the occasion arose.   some drunk hetro plying me with schnapps: *dress up, doll*
what lies did he tell himself, biting his way down to that brass propeller shaft

also abandoned: retiring to miami [though I won't miss the guns or snakes]
or tel aviv [though I wouldn't miss the vipers.   or the snipers]

dreams of a hot husband in a hot tub who'd complain "honey, I shrunk my kids"
and drink fresca all day & rub my feet.   dreams of growing cantankerously old

shouting down the drainspout at a neighbor's brats.   clipping my ruby begonias
haggling over the price of nectarines at the pick 'n pack 'n scrimp 'n save

but climbing always: as up the trellis and overshrouding the eaves, wisteria
spreads in clusters of carcinoma-colored bells.   cascading epithelial light

up the spiral staircase of recombinant chromosomes.   no one wants in these genes
the double helix that swam through the treacherous night: aching to be held again

you couldn't know the disaster this voyage has been.   the *shvimen,* the *shvitzen*
yard by yard the little deaths accrued   [imagine your twin towers over and over and]

out: that glorious sky darkly hung with newspaper lanterns.   scalpel-shaped chimes

—what am I meaning to tell in this cramped space?   bubble suspended in glass—

the reckoning beyond this cargo hold.   dear god, who hears the pounding on the hull

[fortune drives a finned convertible: her blond wig shifts in the wind]

Mondo Trasho (1969, John Waters, dir.)

fortune drives a finned convertible: her blond wig shifts in the wind
in a lab somewhere: technicians spin me in centrifuge.   sudden skidmarks

doctors have no remedy.   they shine their bumpers and wax their hoods
every day I get a little more useless, starting with my shabby feet

the mind [precise once] spills on its favorite outfit: indelible inky wem
wish I'd get stains out.   the cloth of this *schmatte:* my pallium my hide

my, but the gutters bulge with dreck.   landscape flavor du jour: pigsty
no wonder the crones cackle behind my back: *what is it?*   they blurt

: *a cake boy : a bone smuggler : a shim : a smurf : a rice and bean queen
or a greengown?   a monosyllable?   a flesh broker?   a grape picker?   it could be*

*an ass hound.   a rancid flower.   maybe a street mechanic.   probably a peg boy
a flamer   a fister   a flipflop   a floozy   a fluffer   a fooper   a flyer   a frit*

somewhere the shangri-las are singing an endless string of *no no no no no no*
somewhere happy bluebirds fly and even tired heels can take us home

[you'd want to go to the reunion: see]

Parting Glances (1986, Bill Sherwood, dir.)

you'd want to go to the reunion: see
who got heavy.   who got bald.   see

who has ᴋs lesions on the face and listen
to the same old tunes: there'll be a dj sure as anything

you'd want to show off your boyfriend who's spare
as a girlscout cookie.   who drinks to excess

who is immortal who has not tasted
blood from a chalice.   the vampyre's kiss

and whosoever drinks from the cup, they'll tell you
everlasting: they'll say

where did you go when you were lively?
zippers, faces, exile, jackhammer, rawhide, wreck room, the stud

you dress in black leather: color of a cormorant
shared wardrobe passed among siblings.   a masqued ball

lazy last nights on earth: how long has it been since you laid in bed
all day during the workweek.   spewing and rattling like a baby

wearing the loose shift of your skin: all hallows eve
you spook your parents and run through the husks of the fields

remember that once, sneaking out into streets
you sought beyond the boundaries of board games:

life & sorry.   aggravation & trouble (the milton bradley version)
you allowed men to manipulate you.   and were gifted

good boy collectible.   good boy swappable
good boy in a kit with moveable parts: turn him over

see where he's been made.   you laid
in their toy chests.   keepsies

kids everywhere are called to supper: it's late
it's dark and you're all played out.   you want to go home

no rule is left to this game.   playmates scatter like breaking glass
they return to smear the _____.   and you're it

[so the theatre dimmed and reclined. cramped balcony rubbed against my leg]

Far From Heaven (2003, Todd Haynes, dir.)

> . . . leaving the movie before it's over
> with a pleasant stranger whose apartment is in the Heaven on Earth Bldg
> —Frank O'Hara, "Ave Maria"

so the theatre dimmed and reclined.   cramped balcony rubbed against my leg
nibbled popcorn from my buttery lap: what played that particular matinee?

not *les enfants du paradis*.   nothing noble: the re-release of *true grit* or *godzilla v. mothra*
it surprises me not that, years later, in a cassette of home movies, I see me skedaddling

eloped to the cinema—then: eloped *from* the cinema.   how I tore my dungarees
my drawers my shirt my fleshy bottom delicate membrane heart and pouty lips

lime-scented boy of jadite: the green son on a sunday.   fruit of the hidden orchard
to swear off the bottle and onto a stack of *cosmo*s and *esquire*s that it's true

while I collected ribbons for scripture [white ribbon = 5 verses, blue = 25 verses,
and 125 verses for red: color of the blood, my swollen mouth, my blushing penis]

the house teetered: whimpering for nails.   the wiring melted into a scouring pad
a spattering grease fire did what the termites couldn't: pickaxe, crowbar, battering ram

upstairs: the one parent slitting her skirt for sweet thing she brought back from market
the absent other: him at the oriental massage getting *jerkyjerky* and an icy finger up the bum

[I saw this movie twice.   both times I had to pee and missed this part: this parting]

now I wander into someone else's story: ghost light peering from the screen
a lambent young man opens his robe touching himself where he wants me to touch

take my hand and lead me stranger: hot, convulsing, delirious to taste of thy affection

[the atrium of the heart beckons with pendulous lips]

Fantastic Voyage (1966, Richard Fleischer, dir.)

the atrium of the heart beckons with pendulous lips
any seaman would point his submarine inside: sirens sing
an eye flutters.   strewn with carrion: the cliffs

pilot: could I go deep into the plasma of the sea
pull myself from the wreckage.   red tide, white squid
refractile bodies caught in this prismatic stream

surely salvation bilges.   suffers our immersion
as a macrocyte absorbs a viral fret.   into this deep
the whorl of shell and wave flash brilliant consecration

how the anvil beats within the limpet ear.   we drift
red sky at morning over the harbor: the hemoglobin
manta rays sensitive to the current's subtle shift

would the brain allow us entry like a rude thought docking
time to repair the nets and *overboard*   make for the tearducts
grow vast as a seamonkey: in tide pools.   sunlight draining

Bibliography

From the wide window towards the granite shore
The white sails still fly seaward, seaward flying
Unbroken wings

—T. S. Eliot, "Ash Wednesday"

[my lot to spin the purple: that the tabernacle should be made]

                         a song of Mary the mother

my lot to spin the purple: that the tabernacle should be made

with ten curtains of fine-twined linen and scarlet.   and the silk

and the hyacinthine.   even woven with the gold and the undefiled
which is white.   having the true purple for its veil

when the lot fell to me I took up my pitcher and filled it
took the purple upon my fingers and drew out the thread

in shag and floss: in coarse bottoms and in tight glossy skeins
the thrum did wind itself away from me

for a word had entered my womb and leapt inside me

I make the dark pillow where the moon lays its opaque head
I am the handmaid: pricked upon the spindle

the fine seric from the east was brought to me
soft and unfinished.   dyed in the tyrian manner

of purpura and janthina the violet snail.   cowrie and woodcock shell
the spiny hedgehog murex and the slender comb of venus

from betwixt my limbs arachnine the twisting issue I pulled forth

purple the night I felt the stab of the godhead in my side
purple the rot of the silk: its muscardine.   its plague

a raw tuft dwindles beneath me: I feel the tug of a day ravelling
even as such gloom as this winds tight around the wooden reel

would that a potion could blot out the host inside me
grove of oak, chestnut, willow.   a place of skulls.   succubi

a necropolis in me rises.   its colors mingle in the dark: aurora

spinster to throwster: purple my loom spread with the placenta cloth
I put a fine pattern to it: damascene sheaved and lilied

threads thrown in acute manner so that the bee rises on the border
the rose of sharon the cedar the camphire.   calamus and pleasant fruits

and these even dotted with locusts caddis flies and polyphemus moths
a fountain: a garden wattled with reeds upon the weaving

garden to be betrayed in?   a shadow against the breast of the tree

so the flox did luster in mine eye: in the cloth I beheld a fine water
as one might arduously with calender produce: the weft

a wave offering in my hands.   pin that pierces the body

over my lap a spreading wound of purple: purple that puckers and gathers
cloaking my folds of purple.   the swollen vein of a young boy's manhood

purple deep and hopeful.   a scar under the frenum.   a heavy prepuce

a caul.   an umbilical cord.   a wet sluice.   an angry fist.   a broken vessel
a bruise.   a blemish.   a raincloud.   a lesion.   a fissure.   tissue

the ends I took up and selvaged.   this veil shall not fray

and vast the warp of the cloth.   sea of galilee.   tigris euphrates and jordan
flow not as wide as my great bounty: undulant sky above my loom

the shuttle through me: a lance in my side.   a heave in my bowels
how will the temple receive my gift: scab of purple.   pustule.   genitalia

[and a future who?   unfurls above the altar]   the thread the thread the thread

[unsheathed the sword and cut the veil. visible the planet red]

a song at the circumcision

unsheathed the sword and cut the veil.   visible the planet red
he wrapped in cloth: a loaf in offering.   stained: they crushed his grape
now wine trickles from the vats and the barnfloor aches its charge

nectar and pollen pend upon the purpled crown of his stamen
bees encircle the bracteal stalk.   goldfinches: thistledown in their beaks
tanned youths track his scent: rutting bucks with antlers locked

this spillage a petite suffering: sap droplets glister earthward
row that pules and groans to drink.   a pail a pyx a sacred cup
we sip we take our meal and tremble to have this blessing

bloodshed   tender mouths   the philtrum [indentation over the lips
where the seraph's appendage brushed us]   rent garment   skin of silk

a torn membrane makes a fine harp.   we call the sung phrase *ligature*

my love doesn't wind his body in a cloak.   he rears as a lion to the kill
statuesque: a harrow in the field.   the masses venerate his stook
from the steeple skyward reaching peal of bells: lauds and matins

as an athlete wrestles with angels: insists his solid body into aether
so the aether accepts him.   an abraded sky reveals its penetralia

this disquieting dawn the color of festering scabs: a cut that cannot suture
where the banding cloth releases: dehisced petals.   abandoned garments
these naked fishers cast papyrus nets.   this skin the shroud of waking:

[he tastes the air with his tongue. his eyes a gory kitling]

a song of John the Baptist, at the river

They shall take up serpents; and if they drink any deadly thing, it shall not hurt them;
they shall lay hands on the sick, and they shall recover.
— Mark 16:18

he tastes the air with his tongue.   his eyes a gory kitling
his glory: a copperhead's venom.   hemotoxic: eating corpuscles

corpus   redeemer   light   the risen   paraclete   and vine

in the crumpled tissues: moulting snakes tonsure themselves
their papery cowls rattle against the cattails and rushes

at the riverbed colubrid we flurry and wash: nest of vipers
unloosing the latchets of our shoes.   ankles sinking to mud

this canebrake divides and admits us.   reticulated leaves of orchis
erupt in marbled turrets: dry seed spurtles before us on the ground

the musk   the wood   viscosity   the damp   the *the*   the plague
a longing   breech   a rise to cataracts   oratory   anaphylaxis
houseled the heart   unburdened   the chorus   intemperate   unbound

he enters my basin and I swathe his swollen hood.   I bathe his skin
covering the body as rash.   open-lipt praise: I give.   to the wept chancres
[and the ones who kneel in the brush are watching bent and lusting]

187

filled on every side by his exuviae: through the shunt   the heparin lock
catheter   sigmoidoscope   endoscope   intubation   viaticum
I would gladly tear my own shroud at his command: be smeared

& rip.   popped discards: condoms glued to levees.   marking the trails
motocross bikes offroad vehicles and thongs have pressed the path

into the runnel clay.   you can't lose yourself in the floodplain:

go on down: to the wooded reach.   affuse yourself in lymph serene

trouble the water.   trouble the sedge the shore the weeds

down from your loft to the rippling issue.   on your knees unraveled
[aren't I?]   bending to the serpent twisting undulating coiling   [charming?]

shed   flayed open   winding through these grass and fear no deadly hand

[my riches I have squandered. spread with honey]

a song of the prodigal son

my riches I have squandered.   spread with honey
the arval bread in my pocket and nary a farthing

lived for a spell among roaches in a rickety squat
between the alcohol detox and the catholic church

peeled my plump white bottom.   a sauvignon grape
[now exsiccated: the wizened sultana makes no golden cake]

crouched in the gulleys.   wiped with leaves
cooked roadkill: topped with government surplus cheese

snuck in underage at club 21 (2121 21st street, long gone)

wastrel opal-throated bird: a moulting quivers along the pinion

I fear my mucus: its endless volume and amorphous shape
a demon expelling from my lips.   the moon wags its tongue

each dull morning the mirror imagines me a future: older
misshapen forest: stinging adder and sprawling spider

the way to haven seems interminable.   I creak and shuffle
listen, you wilderness: make plain and let me pass

[strange flower in my hands. porphyry shell. clipped wool]

a song of John the Divine with the Holy Prepuce, as in the vision of St. Birgitta

strange flower in my hands.   porphyry shell.   clipped wool
all the dark caves that beckon and terrible mud chambers of the wasp

I touched the raphe of your skin where once it had seamed to you:
amethyst jewels on your crown.   a skullcap upon the crozier of your loins

the old wet clothing of trees lies on the forest floor: naked world
spreading underbrush and tendrils of the new vines moist

once, I buried the soft body of you in my mouth.   licked that hurt place
where they'd cut you   [so long ago: you had put that infancy away]

you grew large inside me.   gifted my lips and throat with a swirling galaxy
milk of the nightsky.   balm from the trembling branches of the poplar

explosion of pale confetti signaling the new year.   the wine is bubbly
the bread, a generous slice.   I will make a ring of this covenant.   I will

bed thee down in a pasture and make a berm of your torso.   I am the marsh
above, a dipper pours thick liquid of your veins: cold now catch you I do

[they hear the clapping of the bell and are afraid]

a song of Lazarus the leper

they hear the clapping of the bell and are afraid
houses untenanted: bedslops spill from the windows
a clump of myrtle.   a scarlet ribbon against the jamb

look to the threshold: house of figs and of affliction
we whom you loved is sick.   maculed and papuled
our extremities knotted and breaking: the cypress bends

we was a beautiful lad once: not putrefactive nor foul
not blistering in the lips and nose.   not punctate: spots scaling
not mammillated with boils.   nor carbuncled.   not ulcerated

we also wore purple and byssus: we had carousing arms
jeweled and sexy.   required no nurse to dress we sores

and we'd easily slake: undeformed, without, *immaculato*

[torch to the stubble of the fields: the harvest has ended]

a song of Mary the Magdalene

torch to the stubble of the fields: the harvest has ended
in the black turf the last cinders wink and loll: the sentries sleeping

remember a time when grain beetled from its stalk.   a fit of ripeness
my body laid out in sheaves to be bound and threshed: broken chaff

all able plowmen leaned their weight upon the till.   furrowed maid
you see how the wheat was bundled: each season, more vetch more tares

untended the parcel fostered scrannel straw.   clods and shale and stone
nipples an earlobe an armpit: in town the statuary already crumbled

the new seed germing: gifting in the storehouse.   comb of honey
a jar of fragrant oil.   physique rid from its abscess: robed in saffronia

in the sky the evening star nudes itself and offers its pallid pelvis
thunderhead: tight scrotum.   my wheat sunders in his fine white teeth

[slightly foetid. foetal and stooped. an afterbirth of rags]

a song of Lazarus of Bethany

slightly foetid.   foetal and stooped.   an afterbirth of rags
myrrh-soaked pus-stained the cracklings the matted hair
but having heels.   I flushed out from my mortared vacuole

then the coins were lifted from my eyes: my lord
because holy is the viscera.   he seals me waxen
plenary dermis: unbroken and unblemished
once more in the trunk and legs orbicular   yet

am I not dust?   when I move through the world
the air receives me.   as did the dirt.   as does his kiss

[the heavenly noise of domesticity murmurs in the kitchen: clink]

a song of the last supper

All love is dead, infected
With plague of deep disdain
—Sir Phillip Sidney

the heavenly noise of domesticity murmurs in the kitchen: *clink*
plates are cleared and stacked on the sideboard.   desserts shimmer
taking coffee black: antidote to the drowse of too much wine

use it up wear it out: ain't nothing left in this old world I care about
a damasked table surrounded by bachelors.   some already parted
regimens of azt, d4t, cryxivan, viracept and early slumber

across the table a handsome bearded man.   his foot glances your shin
you'd sink with him beneath the empire mahogany: lift the perizoma
receive the host: his wounds.   your faith: the sash around his waist

[not a waking mutter. the locusts in cessation]

                    a song in the garden

not a waking mutter.   the locusts in cessation
redstarts dozing and nightjars silent in the tree hollows

longing perches on every branch: acacia myrtle poplar
and a sudden rush of wind kisses with its rough lips

even in the midst of this green and flowering grove: buttonwood
tamarisk silverking and rue.   paradise seems a vacant spot

only the poppies do not slumber: their calyxes turned upward
bid me drink.   and the dove from its secret place cries out

where is my bed?   where is the house in which I was conceived?
am I to lie here among thorns among brambles.   until the daybreak

let me hide: a spring in rock.   let me drink at that hour abundantly

[because I were ready before destruction. bearing the sign of his affliction]

a song of Simon the Cyrene

because I were ready before destruction.   bearing the sign of his affliction
in my laggard arms: the sign was made as the stretching limbs of him

oh, my chasms were afraid of this wooden place and sang over it:
"loose liver, mouth, roots, member"   a bellowing about our head

then we came to rest in the trees as in the end.   there should blossoms be
indeed I hang thickly upon him.   where clear heavens may breathe upon me:
all darkness, all comprehensible night.   let me be humbled in his abundant eyes

I shall want that the drinklings speak upon his heart: his dewy breast
for they have been vinegar and bitterness enough.   ravens among the wheat

"the carrier" I was called.   so did I carry: my hand did not defect.   my sores
who can tell us all about love: a flaying.   the sting of gall upon a hyssop reed

I am putting on his robe.   I clothe his sinew and drape from it and he loves me
here is the garland that moves not upon our head: impales.   razor thorns

and as that crown sits firmly so I sit firm.   and if everything should perish:
as bridegroom reckoned in his likeness I go.   rock, river, permeable flesh

[listen mother, he punched the air: I am not your son dying]

       a stabat mater

listen mother, he punched the air: I am not your son dying
the day fades and the starlings roost: a body's a husk a nest of goodbye

his wrist colorless and soft was not a stick of chewing gum
how tell?   well a plastic bracelet with his name for one.   & no mint
his eyes distinguishable from oysters how?   only when pried open

she at times felt the needle going in.   felt her own sides cave.   she rasped
she twitched with a palsy: tectonic plates grumbled under her feet

soiled his sheets clogged the yellow BIOHAZARD bin: later to be burned
soot clouds billowed out over the city: a stole.   a pillbox hat   [smart city]
and wouldn't the taxis stop now.   and wouldn't a hush smother us all

the vascular walls graffitied and scarred.   a clotted rend in the muscle
wend through the avenues throttled t-cells.   processional staph & thrush

the scourge the spike a stab a shending bile the grace the quenching
mother who brought me here, muddler: open the window.   let birds in

[the ice hadn't cracked. stingy ground: frozen with its hoard of bulbs]

a song of the resurrection

the ice hadn't cracked.   stingy ground: frozen with its hoard of bulbs
how long would march flail us.   bastinado of wind and hail

one morning I rose.   declared an end to winter   [though cold persisted]
convinced that the dogwood wore its quatrefoil splint of convalescence

because the land gives back.   I wanted warmth within its chilled pellicle
radiating blades of cordgrass and wild rye.   the demure false boneset

on the phone with mary my friend: she too persuaded of the thaw
so long withdrawn a blindness had us.   desensitized to sneaping frost

we set out for the bluffs.   surely clover pullulated along the crest
and the air   [no longer chiding]   would teem with monarchs

I had word of a marigold patch: the welkin dotted with butterflies
orange blaze: the deceit of wings and the breeze's pulmonary gasps

the journey stretched.   why hurry?   the promise of the garden enough
the road a pleasant shifting through riparian forest: a windlass a wander

already I have taken a long time to tell you nothing.   nothing awaited us
nothing sprouted out of the ground and nothing flew about the bluffs

brown twigs: a previous splendor born to another season.   now swealing
the wick had held its brief flame: sodden.   the earth received it

whitetails foraged what was left of vegetation: we startled them grazing
one cardinal held watch at the empty beds: injury in the stark white trees

in the town a church kept bare its cross: draped with the purple tunic
we knelt to the wood.   and this I tell you as gospel: the sky shuddered

a bolt shook our hearts on the horizon.   for what seemed an eternity
[for we knew eternity by the silence it brings]   void: then scudding rain

—for Mary Szybist

[A Και Ω]

                a song of the undead

the sepulchre cleaves.   he loosens from the wall and flies
children assemble to him and he whispers "suffer"

this appetite for blood: he enrooted us to
lapping at the wounds upon his sullied fell

now he's scared of pine: the way it pocks his fair skin
in an arcosolium upon a slab he rests his weary teeth

bats flit through the lunette and adore him: blind angels
bridesmaids in black habits.   lifting the veil: *feed*

[came a voice in my gullet: rise up and feast. thunderous]

a song of Simon Peter, concerning his dream

came a voice in my gullet: rise up and feast.   thunderous
a vestment dropping from the violet cope above
not a vestment: a vessel.   amphora the shape of lips

vessel of skin moiled and swollen: a fretting leprosy
and why would I wish a taste?   inside, all manner of beasts
creatures covered in scall charbon and quarter evil

the sea-things one discovers in the net and tosses back
& the coney the camel the tortoise the hare the swine
oysters as well as snails.   those without fins or scales

though I hungered as a sick lass with her empty box
I could not be filled.   not with the tainted reasty lot
in my bowels a raven ruffled its dismal neck and cawed

now I was devout and nothing common or dirty
inside me: not a wild meat not a fruit or spice exotic
for I was a stone: washed in the stream.   I was cut clean

still the air split with want.   the urgent voice seized
because these *are* the pleasures of the world.   *eat*
of the glands I tasted many.   hearts.   lights.   pluck

what had been circumcised fit me.   the uncircumcised too
for nothing was given for my body which was not sacred
the seed the root the tongue and pure blood that cleanses

[when he comes he is neither sun nor shade: a china doll]

a second song of John the Divine, as at the end

when he comes he is neither sun nor shade: a china doll
a perfect orb.   when he comes he speaks upon the sea

when he speaks his voice is an island to rest upon.   he sings
[he sings like france joli: *come to me, and I will comfort you.*   when he comes]

when he comes I receive him in my apartment: messy, yes
but he blinds himself for my sake   [no, he would trip, wouldn't he?]

he blinds *me* for *his* sake.   yes, this actually happens
so that the world with its coins with its poodles does not startle

I am not special: have lied stolen fought.   have been unkind
when I await him in the dark I'm not without lascivious thoughts

and yet he comes to me in dreams: "I would not let you marry"
he says: "for I did love you so and kept you for my own"

his exhalation is a little sour.   his clothes a bit dingy
he is not golden and robed in light and he smells a bit

but he comes.   and the furnace grows dim.   the devil and the neighbors
and traffic along market street: all go silent.   the disease

and all he has given me he takes back.   laying his sturdy bones
on top of me: a cloak an ache a thief in the night.   he comes

202

a song of paradise

to enter that queer niteclub, you step over the spot: sexworker stabbed
reminds me of the chalk outlines on castro street or keith haring's canvases

missing.   beaten.   died at the end of a prolonged illness.   a short fight

phantoms of the handsome, taut, gallant, bright, slender, youthful: go on
the garment that tore: mended.   the body that failed: reclaimed

voyeurs, passion flowers, trolls, twinks, dancers, cruisers, lovers without lovers

here is the door marked HEAVEN: someone on the dancefloor, waiting just for you:

so many men, so little time [miquel brown]
calling all boys by the flirts.   patrick cowley's *menergy*
only the strong survive [precious wilson] or *I will survive* [gloria gaynor]

the flirts' *passion* and roni griffith's *desire*
the boys come to town [earlene bentley]
gloria gaynor's *I am what I am.*   eartha kitt's *I love men*

runaway [tapps].   *seclusion* [shawn benson].   *helpless* [jackie moore]
eria fachin *saving myself* and the three degrees *set me free*
goodbye bad times [oakey & moroder].   *keep on holdin' on* [margaret reynolds]

oh romeo's *these memories* and *the heart is a lonely hunter* [bonnie bianco]
real life's *send me an angel.*   *earth can be just like heaven* [two tons of fun]
yaz: *situation* and *don't go.*   and *why* by bronski beat

give me just a little more time [angela clemmons]
unexpected lovers by lime and *mercy* by carol jiani
let's hang on [salazar] and *maybe this time* [norma lewis]

vivien vee's *give me a break* and her haunting *blue disease*
ashford & simpson's *found a cure.*   *doctor's orders* [carol douglas]
sylvester singing *body strong.*   sylvester singing *stars*

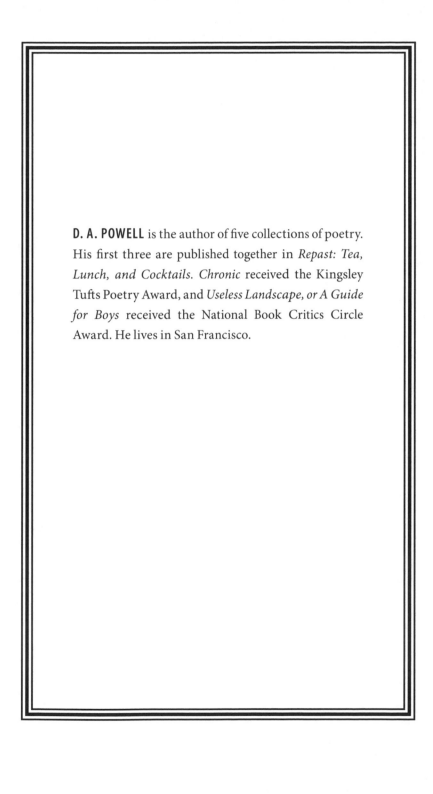

D. A. POWELL is the author of five collections of poetry. His first three are published together in *Repast: Tea, Lunch, and Cocktails. Chronic* received the Kingsley Tufts Poetry Award, and *Useless Landscape, or A Guide for Boys* received the National Book Critics Circle Award. He lives in San Francisco.

The text of *Repast* has been set in Minion, a typeface designed by Robert Slimbach and issued by Adobe in 1989. Book design and composition by Bookmobile Design & Digital Publisher Services, Minneapolis, Minnesota. Manufactured by Versa Press on acid-free, 30 percent postconsumer wastepaper.